Pagan Portals
Where Fairies Meet

Parallels between Irish and Romanian Fairy Traditions

Pagan Portals

Where Fairies Meet

Parallels between Irish and
Romanian Fairy Traditions

Daniela Simina

**MOON
BOOKS**

Winchester, UK
Washington, USA

JOHN HUNT PUBLISHING

First published by Moon Books, 2023
Moon Books is an imprint of John Hunt Publishing Ltd., No. 3 East Street, Alresford
Hampshire SO24 9EE, UK
office@jhpbooks.net
www.johnhuntpublishing.com
www.moon-books.net

For distributor details and how to order please visit the 'Ordering' section on our website.

Design: Matthew Greenfield

UK: Printed and bound by CPI Group (UK) Ltd, Croydon, CR0 4YY
Printed in North America by CPI GPS partners

We operate a distinctive and ethical publishing philosophy in
all areas of our business, from our global network of authors to
production and worldwide distribution.

Contents

Dedicated to those who adamantly required
that I should write this book.

Special thanks to Marin for always challenging me to live as
the strongest version of myself, and to Morgan for shining
light onto the path I thought I'd lost forever.

Foreword

Where Fairies Meet: Parallels between Irish and Romanian Fairy Traditions
By Morgan Daimler

People who are interested in fairies, under any name, tend to immediately look to the Irish and the Celtic nations more generally which is useful but also a kind of tunnel vision that limits the wider picture. Fairies are found, again under diverse names, across Europe and our understanding of these beings and the core beliefs behind them can be enormously enhanced by broadening our study outside that assumed western fringe territory. Rather than narrowing our understanding of these beings down to a small slice of material from a few select cultures we can gain a fuller and deeper grasp of who and what these beings are as well as how human communities related to them by expanding our study outwards. This book does exactly that and does it brilliantly by using the Irish, which are more familiar to a wider audience, in comparison to the Romanian beliefs to not only help the reader understand Romanian fairies but also to see the wider patterns moving behind the entire subject and compare and contrast the various beliefs surrounding fairies in both cultures.

Ireland lies at the western edge of Europe, Romania in the east, with a great stretch of land and culture between them yet when the beliefs about these spirits – the Aos Sidhe, the Zâne – are held up side by side the similarities become apparent and hint at a fascinating shared system of belief. Both cultures' beliefs and practices deserve to be appreciated on their own, of course, but approaching them as this text does, in a way that allows the reader to consider the Irish and Romanian beliefs individually and comparatively, creates a wonderful opportunity to more fully comprehend the nuances of each as well as the obvious overlap. Neither is presented as authoritative over the other but rather the two work seamlessly together so that where they align it seems natural that they do so and where they differ it highlights organic divergences between two diverse cultures.

To understand the beliefs a culture has about fairies is, in many ways, to understand an aspect of that culture itself. What is considered a social norm? What is valued? What is feared? By exploring answers to these questions, as they are expressed in beliefs and practices around fairies, we can see layers to a culture that may not be obvious on the surface. Exploring where the Irish fairy beliefs intersect the Romanian ones shows us some important shared concerns between the two cultures, and discussing where certain beliefs diverge shows us ways that each culture is unique. Fairies in this way are both a deeper feature that holds cultures together and also a way that each can express its own particular understanding of the human world and the world of Fairy that adjoins it.

This book marks a bold step into a cross-cultural inquiry about fairies that seeks to engage the reader beyond the surface stereotypes and delve into the heart of the beliefs, how they exist within their original framework, and what that can perhaps tell us about the core concepts involved. Fairies here are more than just fairies, and more than the Aos Sidhe and Zâne, they are a mirror for a far deeper truth that crosses cultural boundaries and lines on a map.

A Note from the Author

According to my knowledge, no one so far has analyzed side by side Romanian and Irish traditions surrounding fairies, nor underlined the existing parallelism. This alone could be a good reason to write such a study. But the value of "Parallels between Romanian and Irish Fairy Lore and Traditions", as I see it, goes beyond the aforementioned 'first of its kind.'

So, why am I writing this?

Because... There are myriads of viewpoints on fairy: they may be all correct to various degrees, but none of them has a monopoly on truth. There's no such thing as a universally correct and standardized body of knowledge that covers fairies that is flawless, pristinely accurate, or lends itself to precise classifications. (Fairies who fit into neat little boxes? You lost me right there.) Fairies and fairy like-beings are encountered in every culture, and if we accept that cultures are diverse, why not consider that fairies are also diverse? Yet aside from diversity, fairy lore from different cultures show significant contingency points. The existing corpus of material surrounding the Irish fairies and the one that surrounds Romanian fairies is one such example. Why would this matter?

Because... Upon analysis, the existing similarities substantiate the reality of fairy and the veracity of fairy experiences. There's no smoke without a fire, and when bodies of fairy lore from distinct cultures point in the same direction, there must be something true there. Those seeking arguments to support the reality of the fairy phenomena will find plenty in these pages.

Whether from pure curiosity, research-driven interest, or desire to understand fairies and build spiritual paths around relationships with them, a cross-cultural study gives a broader view, and a lot of practical advice. Also, this study allows the reader to develop an integrated perspective on hard-to-get beings, like fairies. (No pun intended in the hard-to-get statement)

Last but not least, fairy lore is ever-evolving with various consequences. The way someone experiences fairies, shapes their perception of fairies thus contributing to further shaping of existing lore. The opposite is also true: the lore shapes expectations, and expectations further shape experience and/or interaction with fairy. But here is also where sheer fabrication and personal experiences come to be presented as genuine lore. This does not make personal experiences less valid; it just doesn't grant them the status of *traditional* lore. I know, we live in the twenty-first century and our understanding of life, nature, and reality in general is different in many regards from how people perceived these, say five hundred years ago. But... many things change on the surface while their core, the essence of what or who they are, doesn't change. There is a reason why children in school study World History: it is not an attempt made by the school system to entice people to live a lifestyle fit for the Middle Ages, but a way to help the present generations understand how the world has changed and the implications of change. This extends to our relationship to fairy traditions past and present: learning about their past helps us to better understand them in the present. The quality of our relationships depend on the degree of understanding, and the degree of understanding depends on what and how much we read, study, and experience. Traditions surrounding fairies act as an intergenerational compass allowing young and old to orient themselves into the ever-changing cultural landscape. As such a compass, fairy traditions allow people to position themselves on the time-space continuum not only through perpetuation of values, but through connecting deeper with subtler realms that surround and interpenetrate consensus reality. This study looks at the lore past and present, and practices of fairy seers from the past which are still in use today. It also gives a glimpse of the author's personal experience growing with her grandmother, a medicine woman and fairy seer, which should provide quite a bit of information of practical use.

You may not be directly interested in Romanian or in Irish fairy lore. But have you considered how do fairies *in your own culture or personal practice* compare to the Irish and Romanian views and experiences of fairies?

Daniela Simina
Alpharetta, U.S.

Introduction

Traditions surrounding fairies act as a cross-generational compass allowing young and old to orient themselves into the ever-changing cultural landscape. As such, fairy traditions allow people to position themselves on the time-space continuum not only through the perpetuation of values, but also through connecting deeper with the subtler realms that surround and interpenetrate consensus reality. Connecting to subtler realms give access to a body of knowledge built upon the record of interactions occurring between our world and the Other. Fairies help us change our attitude in interacting with the world by bringing back the spiritual component.

Romanian and Irish cultures, both of them bearers of rich traditions surrounding fairies, are situated at diametrically opposite locations across the European continent: Romania out to the East, and Ireland far out to the West[1]. Despite geographical separation and development of unique features characteristic to each, Romanian and Irish fairy lore and traditions display a remarkable parallelism. A study of this existing parallelism offers an integrated perspective: side by side analysis of similar elements of fairy lore in Romanian and Irish traditions provides valuable information for researchers of folklore and cultural anthropology who seek to portray fairies and the cultural context of their evolution and manifestation. The aforementioned parallelism is evident when looking at the similarities regarding fairies' physical appearance, types of interactions with humans, the connection with the dead and ancestor figures, and in some cases their origination from ancient gods. In both cultures, the fairies are seen as neither exceedingly benevolent nor exclusively harmful. Each Romanian zâne or Iele, and Irish Aes Side or Na Daoine Maithe, are uniquely themselves, and their particular nature is well described by the word fairy with connotations of unpredictability, change, magical power, danger, and beauty which comes in many forms. Individuality and striking similarities combined, the existing parallelism is intriguing, and worth therefore analyzing. The conclusions may be quite surprising.

Coming up with a definition of fairy that everybody would find acceptable is probably an impossible task. Applied to both Irish and Romanian cultures, the word fairy can be used as a catchall term for several types of beings. Among these types, cross-culturally, some are strikingly similar in the way they appear, what they like, and especially in the way they interact with humans; there are also similarities in the way people approach fairies, and the kind of relationships developing between human and fairy partners.

In the book "Magical Folk: Fairies 500 AD to Present", Dr. Simon Young writes:

A simple but efficient definition is that traditional fairies are 'magical, living, resident humanoids' who dwell exclusively in Britain, Ireland, and some of the lands that British and Irish migrants settled. 'Exclusive' because the continent has its own magical folk, and these have their own characteristics... 'Magical' because fairies do not, of course, obey the normal rules of physics... 'Alive' in the sense that they are not ghosts... 'resident' in that that they are tied to places... Finally, the fairies are 'humanoids'. The vast majority of descriptions are about beings that look like humans or are human-like... they are usually adult- or child-size. (Young, 2018)

According to Dr. Simon Young and upon looking up the etymology of the word fairy, it only makes sense to use it in reference to the Celtic languages speaking cultures and England. While England itself is not among Celtic language speaking cultures, the terms fay and fairy reached there first before spreading into the adjacent territories.

Morgan Daimler explains the etymology of the word fairy.

Fae – also spelled fay – is from the 12th century old French, likely from the older Latin Fata, meaning spirits of fate, and Williams suggests it entered French as a term for Celtic goddesses later shifting to women of supernatural power, then to an adjective meaning roughly enchanting, and finally to the place of Fairyland itself (Williams, 1991). This initial use for the place of Fairy is how the term enters English in the 13th century and we see it developing as both an adjective describing things with the nature of that place as well as a term for beings from that place. Briggs suggests that the initial adjective form may have been fay-erie, to indicate something that was enchanting or had an enchanting nature (Briggs, 1976). In the oldest English sources, we see fairy used as an adjective as well as a noun and this adjectival use continued for hundreds of years. (Daimler, 2020)

In documenting fairy traditions from Southern and Eastern Europe, including Romania, professor emeritus Èva Pòcs describes fairies in these areas as: "Magical beings inhabiting a different dimension." (Pòcs, 1989) Since this definition suits well both Romanian and Irish contexts, I will use the term fairy as the circumstances, and the need for clarity demand.

Beings similar to the Celtic[2] fairies are encountered in probably every culture, and are more or less similar to Celtic and English ones. In Romania they are called *zâne* and/or *iele*. However, when translating from Romanian into English, the term fairy has become habitual. Romanian *zâne* and the Celtic *fairies* are not the exact same thing, but they all fit under the 'fairy' umbrella term. It is beyond the scope of this work to analyze the vastness of fairy population in the Celtic speaking culture. We will focus on the Irish fairies, and their Eastern

European Counterparts, the Romanian zâne. While it is my desire to bring in circulation more the terms *zâne* and *iele* which are virtually unknown outside Romania, occasionally I will still use the generic fairy wherever necessary, to avoid confusion.

Endnotes

1. Romania: Southeastern - Central Europe 45.9432° N, 24.9668° E; Ireland: Northwestern Europe, insular, 53.1424° N, 7.6921° W

2. The term "Celtic" is used in reference to Celtic languages speaking cultures as they are known today: Ireland, Scotland, Wales, Cornwall, Island of Man, and Bretagne region in France

Chapter 1

Fairies in Irish and Romanian Lore

Irish and Romanian lore give quite similar descriptions of Sidhe and Zâne /*Zuneh*/[3]. Same as the Irish avoiding using the word fairy, Romanians also prefer to avoid in most cases the name *zâne* opting instead for *iele* /*yeh-leh*/, a pronoun that translates roughly as *They or Themselves*. One theory links the name *zâna* to *zena*, a word of Dacian origins[4]. The name *zena*, meaning hemlock, alludes to the dangerous nature of zâne.

> The word 'zena' is listed by Dioscorides as a Dacian word with the meaning 'hemlock'. Looking further into this word's etymology we find Skt. jyanay-, Av. zyanay-, zyana-, 'to overcome, conquer, weaken', with a reconstructed as PIE *ĝiena, *ĝeie- 'subjugate, overpower, oppress'. (Detschew 1976) Thus the argument can be made that the Dacian word 'zena' meaning 'hemlock', presents another etymology for the Romanian *zâna*, plural *zâne*, feared powerful fairies, that could 'subjugate' 'oppress' people, damage their health or cripple them, if not revered. (Chelariu, 2020)

Occasionally, things get more complicated: while in some contexts iele and zâne are used interchangeably, most times, iele is used to describe specific fairy beings who act inimically toward people, while zâne is descriptive of benevolent fairies. Other names used especially in reference to the less friendly and more dangerous iele, are: Vântoasele (The Stormy Ones), Binecuvântatele (The Blessed Ones), Albele (The White Ones), Luminatele (The Bright Ones). The Irish tradition recommends euphemisms such as Na Daoine Maithe, meaning The Good People, and Good Neighbors, Gentry, Fair Folk (fair has the connotation of noble and it is unrelated to skin tone), and Shining Ones. Romanian lore and stories portray iele/zâne as being of average human size or taller, and usually very beautiful. While Rusalii and Sânziene are the major groups of fairies in Romanian tradition, there are other fairy beings, zâne, not specifically relegated to any of these two categories.

The Sânziene are noted for their passionate nature, their connection to solar energy, and solar/summer symbolism. (Kligman, 1981; Eliade, 1955; id. 1975, Pócs, 1989; id. 2018)

As fairies of flowers and medicinal plants, the Romanian *zâne* are spirits of the earth, helpers of the Great Goddess, Ileana Simziana, feared and revered by women. (Chelariu, 2020)

Rusalii are the dark counterpart of the bright Sânziene (Kligman, 1981; Pócs, 1989; id. 2018;) Although the feast of Rusalii precedes that of Sânziene by only about six weeks[5], and is associated with summer time, the Rusalii themselves are quite sinister and decidedly more dangerous than Sânziene. Aside from Rusalii and Sânziene, Romanians know other zâne, who are connected with nature, natural phenomena, and places. Romanian fairy lore from the last two hundred years is populated with nature-connected zâne, which will be discussed later in this book. While they do appear more often in relatively recent tales, the nature-connected zâne are not modern fiction, but archaic elements preserved in oral folklore. From the tales collected and rewritten by folklorists and writers of the last two centuries, nature fairies made their way into modern and contemporary narratives. (Pócs, 2018; id. 1989; Mawr, 2021; Urechia, 1904/1978; Creangā, 2017; Slavici, 2017; Eminescu, 2017; Eliade, 1976)

Romanian tales feature fairy queens who appear dressed in the traditional garb of country women (Creanga, 2017; Chelariu, 2021), or wearing outfits made of unconventional materials such as butterfly wings and spider web silk (Urechia,

1978). Other times fairy queens and their retinue have luxurious wardrobes and live in castles. (Mawr, 1861/2021; Urechia,1978; Stanescu,1892)

In Irish mythology the Aes Side are believed to be the Tuatha Dé Dannan, the old gods who, after the Milesians invasion, went to live into the mounds alongside the already existing fairy-beings (Lebor Gabála Érenn, 65-95, The Milesians; Evans-Wenz, 1911). The Aes Side appear to be human size or taller, and very beautiful. For example, in the Táin Bó Cúailnge, Lugh himself comes to the aid of his son, Cú Chulainn. Lugh shows up as "A great, well-favoured man..." (Dunn, 2005) In the same text, Táin Bó Cuailnge, Morrigan appears to Cú Chulainn as an exceptionally good-looking woman.

> Cuchulainn saw a young woman coming towards him, with a dress of every colour on, and her form very excellent. (Dunn, 2005)

In the Irish Otherworld, the old gods from among the Tuatha Dé Dannan account for only one part of inhabitants, forming probably an elite that includes fairy queens and kings. However, not all among the fairy kings and queens are known to come from among the Tuatha Dé Dannan. (Daimler, 2019), and the Irish fairy Otherworld[6] has a great variety of inhabitants. First, in the Faith of the Children on Tuirenn story which is part of the Cath Maige Tuired epic, Lugh brings with him the fairy cavalcade which he leads in the battle against Fomorians.

> And he was Lug Lamh-fada [i.e. Lug of the long arms and furious blows], and [his army was] the Fairy Cavalcade from the Land of Promise... (O'Curry, 1863)

This informs the reader that there *were* already fairy people in the mounds who possessed significant military power which they lent to the Tuatha Dé Danann under Lugh's command.

Second, not all the inhabitants of the síde (fairy mounds) were queens and kings, or warriors. Na Daoine Maithe, the euphemism meaning The Good People, includes fairy beings from all walks of life. Na Daoine Maithe is synonymous to the Aes Side, and includes monarchy, royal courts and retinues, alongside people living simple lives, farming, rearing children, etc. The Aes Side live similarly to humans in many ways. They need food, various tools, and animals, which they borrow or steal from humans. They live in a world parallel to the human world, and at certain times and in certain places these worlds bleed into each other.

Encounters with members of Na Daoine Maithe are described in stories collected by Eddie Lenihan, Lady Wilde, W.B. Yeates, and Evans-Wentz. Accounts of fairy encounters and surrounding lore are preserved in the School Collection on Duchas.ie. For those not familiar, this is a project run in Ireland in the 1930s, and involved school-aged children collecting stories, in an attempt to preserve the treasures of Irish folklore still in existence.

One example among many is the account of a fairy who knocks at a door in the middle of the night asking for the teenage girl in the household to accompany him. He appears as a well-dressed gentleman riding a fine horse, and the people in the house where he stops do not recognize him as a fairy. They cry bitterly, believing that a strange nobleman is taking away their daughter. Shortly after, the family is amazed to see their girl returning, and even more amazed to hear that she had been taken to a fairy house to assist a fairy woman in childbirth. (Lenihan, 2003) The domestic landscape that the girl encounters in Fairy is similar to her everyday reality, where women give birth and need, maybe, husbands rush in the middle of the night to get a midwife.

Whether kings and queens, noblemen, or inhabitants of Fairy

without any particular ranks, both Romanian and Irish fairy people love sports, music, dance, and party. Examples abound.

Endnotes

3. Zâne are the Romanian fairy beings comparable in certain aspects to the Irish Sí or, Sidhe

4. Prior to the Roman conquest (102CE), the territory of modern Romania was occupied by the kingdom of Dacia.

5. The feast of Rusalii occurs 50 days after Easter. Once a Pagan holiday, the Feast of Rusalii survived in Christian guise as Pentecost. Most likely the original date was changed to fit the Christian calendar to avoid obliteration by the Church, or for the Church to adopt it because the local population would not give up on fairy beliefs and related practices.

6. A world parallel to consensus reality, where fairies, gods, and similar beings' dwell.

Chapter 2

Fairies and Sports

Playing sports is more popular with the Irish than it is with Romanian fairies. Irish lore abounds in stories about fairies getting humans to either act as judges or directly participate in hurling and Gaelic football. In the story "Refereeing a Fairy Hurling Match", Eddie Lenihan describes a quite typical case of human-fairy interaction that occurs around sports.

A man walks home at night. While passing by a fairy mound, in the moonlight, he sees a fairy man on the path. The fairy man asks the traveler to judge a game of hurling, which he passionately describes as very important. The man wearily agrees. He knows that a refusal would be considered impolite and attract the fairies' wrath. The game begins and the man arbitrates the encounter to the best of his abilities. He is concerned, however, that if he announces one team as the winner, the other team will become angry and vengeful. Not wanting to be caught in the middle, and with a little bit of luck, the man is able to signal the end of the game about two minutes early, when the score was even. His worries dispel as the players on both teams' praise and congratulate the man for having judged their best game yet. The man goes home and decides to never again walk that road after dark.

However, not all encounters that fairies have with humans in the context of playing sports ends well for the human protagonist.

There is another account on Duchas of a man who saw the fairies hurling in a field and went to join them only to be kept playing until he almost died of exhaustion. (Morgan Daimler, "Fairy Help, Fairy Harm")

The stories not only narrate the encounter between a human and a group of fairies, but also makes clear the passion Na Daoine Maithe have for sports, their competitiveness, and the enjoyment they get from playing.

While the theme of fairies playing sports is not present in Romanian folklore, there are accounts of zâne challenging humans to perform seemingly impossible tasks. The challenge often takes the aspect of competitions where the human protagonist is pressured to outperform the fairy challenger. In such competitions the stakes are really high, involving a special gift, a priceless possession, the safety or health of a loved one, or the very life of the human challenger.

One such account is featured in the book "The Fairies of the Stag Valley"[7], a collection of stories curated by Nestor Urechia, published in 1904. Within this collection, "Itty-Bitty" [8] is the story of a young man of exceptional wit and courage who is cursed by one of the Rusalii to never grow taller than a young child. Because he is kind as much as he is smart and brave, he gains the sympathy of a fairy who tips him on how to undo the curse. Itty-Bitty is tasked to steal a tuft of hair from the powerful and dangerous Rusalie who cursed him in the first place. The Rusalie shape-shifts into a squirrel, and it is nearly impossible to catch alive. The clever Itty-Bitty tricks the Rusalie turned squirrel to come close enough, and he cuts off her brow the much-needed tuft of hair. The spell breaks and Itty-Bitty is rewarded for his bravery and cleverness. This story in particular, albeit being re-written and bordering on folkloresque, carries on archaic elements still encountered in the oldest surviving fairy narratives, namely, those elements of humans engaging in some form of competition against zâne.

Endnotes
7. Romanian, original, "Zânele din Valea Cerbului
8. Romanian, original, "Prichindută"

Chapter 3

Fairy Entertainment: Music, Dance, and Party

Romanian and Irish fairies alike, have an established reputation for loving music, dance, and partying. In Romania, the Sânziene dance outside on the Night of Sânziene, and the Iele are out on the days of Rusalii, dancing and singing. Occasionally, outside their special days, the zâne can be encountered randomly in places such as fields, meadows, hills, forests, and near bodies of water. They sing and play instruments, and their music is exquisite. Iele, Sânziene, and other zâne have their own skilled musicians, but they also appreciate human talent. It is not uncommon for those young men who are well-known for their skills with the *scripca*[9], flute, and bagpipes to be "borrowed" or hired by fairies. Almost always, these men return to the human world. They may be rewarded with money, a new instrument that is superior to the one they had before, or with blessings that may carry over throughout one's life and maybe, in future generations. Oftentimes, the returned musicians are required to keep secret the source of their gifts. Failing to do so results in bad luck, maiming, or death. (Pòcs, 2018; Talos, 2002)

Another category of fairies, the dangerous Sântoaderi, walk around villages on their specific night. Music and the sound of iron shod feet signal their presence, and warn people to stay inside their houses. Men (Kligman, 1981; Talos, 2002)

In the story "The Slippers of the Twelves Princesses", collected on commission by Elizabeth B. Mawr for Queen Victoria, twelve fairies, initially introduced as princesses, attend nocturnal balls where they dance until their slippers tear apart. (Mawr, 1861/2021) But outside castles with elaborated gardens and sumptuously decorated banquet halls, zâne also have their own

12

meadows, glens, places in the fields or nearby waters where they gather to dance oftentimes by moonlight. (Urechia, 1904/1978; Pòcs, 2018; Kligman, 1981; Talos, 2002) In "Zânele din Valea Cerbului"[10], the zâne guardians of the valley gather at night to share stories, and dance (Urechia, 1904). According to local folklore, humans are not permitted to watch the zâne dancing, and spying almost always ends badly for the human. The places where the zâne dance are easily recognizable because of the circles of brown grass left behind. It is considered dangerous to step inside such circles. Solitary trees growing in the fields and particularly beautiful tree specimens in groves and glens are known as gathering places for fairies, and therefore are treated with utmost respect. Fairy trees are generally avoided except on specific holidays when offerings made to zâne are left at their roots, or for the rare occasions of fairy-related rituals. (Vivod, 2018, Talos, 2002)

Irish fairies show their appreciation for music and musicians in ways similar to the Romanian zâne. Na Daoine Maithe take away musicians which they sometimes reward with mastery of skills, money, and blessings that may carry down through generations. (Daimler, 2017) Same as their Romanian counterparts, the Irish musicians taken into Fairy are required to keep secret the details of their Otherworldly encounters under threats of terrible consequences. Fairy music is unmistakable in its harmony, rapturously beautiful, and very difficult to reproduce. Occasionally, humans hearing fairy music try to reproduce it at public events against fairy consent which ends badly for the musician. (www.duchas.ie[11]) Granting skills, gifting instruments, and sometimes money, are customary rewards that fairies in Ireland would give musicians. (Lenihan, 2003)

In the account given by Mr. J. Blair from Donegal, Ireland, once a year fairies like to gather by the fire in human households and read books. Mr. Blair also mentions a specific location, a glen on Argery Hill, where fairies come every night to dance. (The School Collection, www.duchas.ie[12])

In Ireland, fairies party often. At fairy parties there's always an abundance of food, and food itself is of the most appealing kind. However, stumbling upon a fairy party sounds much better than it actually is. People who join fairy parties and partake of fairy food are feted to either remain in Fairy forever, or die soon. In the account "Local Happenings - The Fairy Party", three children coming home from school cross through a glen where they see a large party going on. There's plenty of food laid out on a white table cloth. At the gathering, with all the ladies and gentlemen dressed in their finest, the children are invited to partake in some food. Two out of the three children eat, while the third one stubbornly refuses. Once at home, the children tell their families about the "lucky" encounter with a partying crowd. Shortly after, the two children who ate from the food at the party died, at which point fairy involvement was suspected. The third child, the one who refused to touch the food, continued to live, and at the time this story was collected, she was sixty years old. (www.duchas.ie[13])

Endnotes

9. Romanian version of the Irish fiddle.
10. "The Fairies of the Stag Valley", translated from Romanian.
11. "The Piper's Stone at Conuovree" https://www.duchas.ie/en/cbes/4742112/4736992
12. https://www.duchas.ie/en/cbes/4493721/4414124
13. https://www.duchas.ie/en/cbes/4922007/4917632

Chapter 4

Fairies' Connection to Natural Features and Phenomena

The majority among the Romanian fairies have strong nature associations. The lore abounds in examples of fairies specifically known for their roles involving seasons, natural elements, landscape features, and places. A few such examples are Zâna Vijeliilor, the Storm Fairy, Codreana Sânziana, Fairy of the Green Woods, Muma Pădurii, Old Mother of Woods, Ileana Sânziana, fairy reigning over midsummer days and wild flowers.

The Sânziene and their queen, Ilena Sânziana, are connected to medicinal and magical herbs which they bless on specific dates; their name is homologous to the flowers, Sânziene – Lady's bedstraw *(Galium verum)* and Yellow bedstraw *(Cruciata laevipes)*. The Sânziene are reputed as benevolent toward humans unless they get offended in which case, they could be merciless.

> ...the Rumanian *rusalii* who appear in *Rusalia* Week before Whitsuntide ...and also bring storms and hail. (Pòcs, 2018)

A group of zâne known as Vântoasele, The Ones of the Winds, take the appearance of whirlwinds or travel in the middle of whirlwinds.

> One main characteristic of the fairies under study is their appearance in a *wind* or in a *whirlwind*. They live "up in the sky", they direct the clouds, their flight is accompanied by eddies, they make whirlwinds, or their dance is a whirlwind itself. (Pòcs, 2018)

Some zâne, while occasionally appearing in the guise of saints, act as patrons over specific days of the week. One such example is Sfânta Duminică who, in the Story of Harap Alb, reveals her identity as the Queen of Fairies in addition to her role as patron of Sunday, a holy day in Romanian culture. (Creangă, 1877)

There are also mine-dwelling fairies who, depending on how they are treated, can be helpful or utterly hostile to humans. A quite well-known story, "The Golden Rose ", is one such example. A young mine-worker has one glass too many, and in an argument with his fiancée, curses their relationship. He goes as far as vowing to marry her only when roses will bloom deep down inside the mine shaft. To make things worse, the young man invokes the fairy guardian of the mine as a witness to his vow. Shortly after, the girl and the young man are struck with remorse, but apparently there's nothing they can do. The girl intervenes, and persuades the mine fairy to give the contrite young man a second chance. Through honesty and kindness, the man finds favor with the mine fairy who leads him to discover, deep down in the mine, an enormous vein of gold in the shape of a rose. He is consequently reunited with the girl he loves, and promises to the fairy to be very mindful of his words and conduct from then on. The story highlights few essential elements which are typically present in fairy-human interaction: the words have binding power, and courage, kindness, and honesty are of paramount importance. (Spariosu, Benedek, 1994)

Mine fairies can ask for a blood price in order to reveal hidden treasures. They also reward bravery and fairness, but do not hesitate to exact their tribute from unscrupulous and greedy individuals. In the tale "Three Partners", a mine fairy appears in the form of a scruffy cat who approaches three miners, one by one. "Give me a man's head, and I'll give you plenty of gold", the fairy entices the first partner, Francis. The cat haunts him for three days, always appearing at noon and sunset, repeating its request. Francis doesn't give into fear, or greediness. However, the other two men mining together, Mathew and Andrew, are quickly persuaded by the cat's promise for gold, and they plan to kill Francis. The mine fairy maneuvers things in such a way that Mathew and Andrew have the illusion they killed Francis. Blinded by greed, Mathew goes on killing Andrew, steals his gold, and then goes to report to the police that his two partners killed each other in an argument. The cat awakens Francis, who lost his senses when his two partners had struck him with a shovel. He sees Andrew lying dead in a pool of blood, and panics. The mine fairy tells him not to fear, but to get as much gold as he can carry and run away from there immediately. As soon as Francis leaves the mine, Mathew returns accompanied by police. However, all they can see are thick cobwebs stretching everywhere, a few rusty pickaxes and a disheveled mine cart, all showing that no one had been there in ages. There are no bodies, no gold, and none of the partners' mining equipment. The police declare there is nothing to investigate, and Mathew goes insane. (Spariosu, Benedek, 1994)

The tale "Three Partners" illustrates the power that zâne – mine fairies in this case – have to hurt or help, their grim side, and the dire consequences that people face when interacting with fairy guardians of places.

Fairies guarding forests demand respect. Treating the woods with disrespect may prove fatal. In "The Forest " tale, a group of woodcutters gather around the fire to decide how much more they should cut considering that they had already reached their quota for the season. Before officially beginning their council, the elder among woodcutters first makes an offering to the zâne guardians of the forest. "First the old man poured a few drops of brandy on the ground. "Here, this is for you…. Please don't harm us." The bottle goes around, and when it returns to the elder, he pours out the last bit of brandy asking the wood fairies for protection. The man then reminds his crew that throughout the entire season they enjoyed good health and no accidents had befallen any of them. He reminds them about the danger of angering the local zâne if they keep cutting. While the older men agree with him, the younger ones would have none of it. One woodcutter and his two sons split from the group and return to work. The older son gets injured and dies from bleeding shortly after. The elder again asks the wood fairies to be content with one man, and allow them to go unharmed. But the boy's father, blinded with grief, wants revenge. He challenges the fairy of the place, and spitefully sets fire to one old and large tree. The tree burns out in a very strange manner: not one single ember rolled away, not one leaf on the ground caught fire. The father and the remaining son rush toward the woods and begin hacking with their axes. The rest of the men run to stop them, but are unable to move or speak, held in place by an invisible hand. They all see a tall and slender figure walking behind the son and touching his shoulder. At this point the axe rotates into the youngster's hands and his arms flex pulling the axe's edge toward his own face. The boy drops dead with the axe stuck in his forehead. The father then chases after someone visible only to himself, and waving the axe rushes into the nearby river. A raft appears out of nowhere with a tall and slender figure standing on it. Logs, stacked up near the water, come loose and roll into the stream, crushing the man as he tries to climb onto the raft. All the while, the tall figure remains impassible, and once the man is torn to pieces and his blood dyes the waters red, it vanishes leaving the empty raft floating away. (Spariosu, Benedek, 1994)

It goes without saying that the fairy guarding the woods in Romania can be ruthless when treated with disrespect. They gladly accept offerings, brandy in this case, but will not hesitate to claim lives when ignorant humans express doubt about their existence and power.

Last but not least, the hags, who are discussed in detail in the next section, are known in Romanian lore for holding dominion over dark and deep forests, connection to winter or wintery weather, and to landscape features such as rock formations.

In the Irish lore, fairy queen Aoibheall is described as holding multiple roles, among which is wielding powers over elements. She is known as "...Aoibheann the Lovely One, a queen and protective spirit of the land...", a description that illustrates her connection to the land itself. Also Aoibheal can command rains and storms. In the lore, the place where she made her abode is identifiable, "...up the top of Crag Hill, surrounded by forest, where Aoibheall used to sit...From there she could command the weather, brewing up storms and high wind when needed to protect her people..." (Marshall, 2013)

An Dagda, king of the Tuatha Dé, and king of fairies in Ireland, owns a magical harp named Daur da Bláo, The Oak of Two Blossoms, and Coir Cethar Chuir, The Four Angle's Music. Through playing his harp An Dagda turns the seasons. He is also connected with shaping the land in various ways, and can control the passing of time, all of which will be detailed in the next section.

Encounters with Each Uisce, the water horse, are considered very dangerous. Water horses are shapeshifting fairies who can take the form of horses or humans as they wish. In their horse form, they are exceptionally beautiful animals and one may be tempted to catch one if found roaming free. However, the attraction for water is irresistible and the water horse will return to the lake it came from at the first opportunity. If the human stands in the way, he will be almost certainly killed, as it is told in "The Story about a Water Horse" (duchas.ie[14]). The story is that of a man who finds a water horse by a lake. The horse follows him home and for a while stays with the man. After a while, the man takes the horse to the lake to drink, at which time the horse wants to jump into the water. The man gets trampled while trying to restrain the horse, who disappears into the lake never to be seen again.

A more sinister aspect of Each Uisce is their appetite for humans. The fairy horse may lure men to try to ride them, and once the rider is on their back the horse makes it to the water where it drowns the victim and eats it. "Folk Tales – The Water Horse" (duchas.ie[15]) is the story of a man who captures a water horse and brings it home. He trains the horse, and then allows his young son to ride it. When they come close to the sea the boy tries to halt the horse but cannot. He can't get off the horse's back either once they get into the water. In the end, the horse drowns the boy and eats him.

There are a few stories about water horses becoming good companions to people and work the fields like any other horse, but they will return to the water at the first chance and there is nothing to stop them. However, the majority of the existing body of lore describes the prey-predator dynamic going on between people and water horses.

Known as Rón or Roane in Irish, they are fairy women who shape shift into seals. The sea is their home. On land they take their seal coat off and turn into women. If the coat is stolen or lost, they cannot shape shift back again into a seal. (Daimler, 2020) There is no equivalent for the Roan in Romanian fairy lore, except for mermaids or women of the fairy inhabiting rivers. There are no accounts of long-term relationship of any kind between fairies associated with bodies of water and humans, except for sightings and occasional, brief interaction.

Fairy queen Áine has close associations to Lough Gur. Her castle is said to be in that lake, and she still appears sitting nearby and combing her beautiful hair. The story "Áine and the Fer Fí" describes a healing ritual involving the "Áine the bean-sidhe and spirit of Lough Gur." (duchas.ie[16])

Endnotes

14. https://www.duchas.ie/en/src?q=The+water+horse&t=Cbes Transcript
15. https://www.duchas.ie/en/src?q=The+water+horse&t=Cbes Transcript
16. https://www.duchas.ie/en/cbes/4922068/4849492

Chapter 5

From Gods to Fairies

There are a few examples in both Romanian and Irish fairy lore that suggest a deity status initially held by certain fairy beings. In Romania, the most popular among such demoted deities are Ileana Cosânzeana and Fāt Frumos. Fāt Frumos is the protagonist of countless tales. His name translates as Handsome Lad. During the twentieth century, many stories involving Fat Frumos have increasingly shifted from folklore into the folkloresque. However, the older versions of these more recent, folkloresque, tales contain elements that speak clearly of a solar figure, and possibly a demoted sun or sky deity. "Fāt Frumos Cu Pārul De Aur", "Handsome Lad with Golden Hair", (Ispirescu, 1872) preserves the ancient theme of a cosmic god, his relationship to humans, fairies, and the landscape. In the story, the precise identity of Handsome Lad is not clear. Initially he appears as a human, but as the story advances, Handsome Lad wields supernatural powers and is attributed fairy status. On the battlefield, Handsome Lad's simple presence scares away the enemy who runs away at his shining radiance, a possible analogy of the sun prevailing over storm clouds. Handsome Lad wears an outfit embroidered with celestial bodies: the sun on the chest, the moon on the back, and the stars on the sleeves. He rides a magical winged horse that can fly so high that Handsome Lad "touches the moon with his hands, the sun with his feet, and from among the stars, he chooses some to make himself a crown" (Creangā, "Harap Alb'", 1877).

In "Povestea Porcului", "The Story of the Pig" (Creangā, 1877) Handsome Lad's pregnant wife cannot give birth until she is reunited with her lost husband. Handsome Lad, originally a solar deity, is kidnapped and hidden away by an old woman with dark powers. The old woman is probably a personification of Winter. She separates Handsome Lad from his pregnant beautiful wife who is most likely a representation of the fertile earth, dormant in winter time. The wife finds her long lost husband after traveling all the way across, "to the other end of the world"[17]. The story may be a metaphor for the sun again warming the earth, after the long months of Winter, and under his benevolent warmth new life is born.

These tales which portray Fat Frumos as a fairy man rising to king status preserve a much older layer of meaning, that of Fāt Frumos, once being a solar deity or sky god with agency over elements, celestial bodies, and the earth itself. As already stated, he crowns himself with a crown made of stars which explicitly shows both he degree and dominion of his power. Like many other ancient gods, Fāt Frumos survives the passing of time and the changes in religious landscape, shining time and again from the realm of Fairy.

An Dagda, whose name translates as "the good god", is a pivotal figure in Irish myth and fairy lore. An Dagda excels in everything: martial skill, healing, bardic skill, and magic, are all in his purview. Daithi O'hOgain refers to An Dagda as a solar deity, which makes sense given that he can change the seasons with his magical harp. But An Dagda also shapes the land when his staff drags on the ground leaving behind him a trench. (Stokes, 1891) In Tochmarc Emire, 'The Wooing of Emer' An Dagda redeems the plain of Muirthemne from underneath waters by removing a giant turtle. He appears thus related not only to sun and weather, but to land and water features as well. These speak of An Dagda as a cosmic deity with a role in creating landforms and water features.

By the power he wields as cosmic deity, An Dagda can control the passing of time. In the story "The Wooing of Etain " An Dagda compresses the passing of nine months into one single day.

Óengus was conceived when Dagda fell in love with Eithne, also called Boann, the goddess of the Boyne and the wife of Elcmar of the Brug. The Dagda sent Elcmar on an errand to Bres, and in the meantime used his magic to make one day last nine months. At the end of this time, Óengus was born. (Mary Jones, 2003)

When the Tuatha Dé Danann withdraws into the fairy mounds, An Dagda negotiates with the conquering Milesians the offerings they have to make to the Aes Sidhe in exchange for the pastures and cattle to be fertile again. People who have settled on the land have to pay homage to An Dagda, as humans throughout history have propitiated gods of land with offerings.

An Dagda emerges clearly as leader among the Aes Sí, the People of the Mounds, a power to be reckoned with and to whom humans must give part of the harvest, if they are to live in Ireland. A later tale mentions An Dagda explicitly as fairy king.

Fergne said to the Dagda that he was the "fairy king of Erinn" and he implored Dagda to send for the fairy king of Munster, Bodb, whose knowledge was known far and wide. (Aslinge Oenguso)

Textual evidence supports therefore An Dagda's relegation from god status to that of fairy king, or his dual capacity as both deity and fairy king.

Ileana Cosânzeana, or Ileana Sânziana, is the best known and by far the most loved among the fairies populating Romanian folklore. Ileana Sânziana is the protagonist of numerous fairy tales where she appears related to Fat Frumos, either as his sister or as his bride. (Chelariu, 2021) Her name, Sânziana, is eponymous to the fairies known as Sânziene and to the flowers these fairies are connected to[18]. Ileana Sânziana is known in lore as Doamna Zânelor, meaning the Queen of Fairies. Ileana

Sânziana and her zâne, the powerful yet benevolent Sânziene, are most active during their eponymous holiday. The celebration begins on the night of June 23rd, which is called the Night of Sânziene. Huge bonfires are lit on top of hills, and young men swirl around carrying torches. The circular pattern shining in the dark is reminiscent of the Sun, and speaks of the origins of the holiday and its protagonists, the Sun and solar deities worshiped in pre-Christian times.

In ancient times, the people living in the area of modern-day Romania followed a religion which included the worship of the Sun or solar deities. Ileana Sânziana and her retinue of zâne can be understood as survivors of those times and traditions; the solar queen Sânziana or Cosânzeana could be a solar deity aside from being a fairy queen. The day following Midsummer Night, June 24th is the Feast of Sânziene. Women wake up early to gather the herbs that zâne blessed the night before when flying over fields and woods. On this day it is customary for people to gather for picnics, and leave out offerings for Sânziene and their queen. The offerings and the way they are presented follow very specific rules. Only white items of the best quality one can afford are acceptable. A white tablecloth is laid out, and a platter is made for Sânziene; cheese, butter, milk or yogurt, hard boiled eggs, and white bread are traditional offerings. If roast chicken is being offered, it has to come from a white chicken especially killed and cooked for the occasion. Fresh water and a glass of wine are always welcome. Strangers showing up unexpectedly are invited to join the party, because they could be actual fairies. At the end of the picnic, the offerings are left by a tree, near a crossroad, or near a body of water. (Chelariu, 2021, Pòcs, 2018, Vivod, 2018)

Some sources mention Ileana Sânziana connected to the moon, thus complementing the solar Fāt Frumos, while the zâne in her retinue acquire in this interpretation the association to stars. (Chelariu, 2021)

"The best-hearted woman who ever lived", this is how Irish

lore refers to Áine, the goddess and fairy queen who people still celebrate on Summer Solstice or Midsummer[19] (O'hOgain, 2006) Around this date, Áine and her retinue, and other fairies as well, travel and make their presence felt in the human world. On the night of Midsummer/Solstice they are said to mingle with the crowds celebrating; so fairy encounters are quite likely at this time, and several stories exist about fairy encounters occurring on this occasion. One such story mentions a group of boys roaming around a hillside on Midsummer Eve, chatting as they walk. The discussion revolves around fairies. One of the boys reminds the group to talk respectfully and not make jokes about Na Daoine Maithe, but the others in the group laugh at him. The boys reach a certain tree on the hillside; they sit to rest, but fall asleep. Fairies come and turn the disrespectful boys into horses whom they raced mercilessly along the country all night long. The one boy who believed in fairies and acted respectfully, was given a beautiful horse to ride through the night to his enjoyment. The boys are brought back, and in the morning they all talk about having had a strange and unusually vivid dream. However, there is one intriguing detail: the boys who didn't show respect to fairies, all 'dreamed' of being turned into horses and raced to exhaustion the whole night. Upon waking up their bodies are terribly sore and bruised. The one boy who did show respect to fairies, tells others about his wonderful dream where he was given a splendid horse to ride and had a great time throughout the night.

There is also the story of a girl encountering Áine herself during a Midsummer celebration. Áine shows her the fairies dancing on the hill, and invites the girl to join. The girl declines the invitation, leaves unharmed, and tells her story that becomes part of the current body of existing fairy lore and stories about Áine.

These examples of fairy encounters on or around Midsummer are by no means singular. Many such stories can be found in the works of Eddie Lenihan, Walter Evans Wentz, Lady Wilde, and in the School Collection on duchas.ie, to name only a few sources.

On Midsummer, the night of June 23rd, bonfires are lit on hilltops in Áine's honor, and people gather to party, eat, drink, and dance. Young men jump over fire to show their prowess, and as tradition has it, to ensure strength and health in the months to come. To do divination for love, couples jump over fires holding hands; if partners let go of each other's hand while leaping over fire, it is said the union won't last. Fires are lit in Áine's honor, but also for apotropaic purposes considering that not all fairies are benevolent toward humans. Depending on local traditions and beliefs, herbs for medicinal or magical purposes are gathered either on the morning after Summer Solstice or on Midsummer. It is said that in passing the fairies have touched these herbs rendering them particularly powerful. Áine has solar associations, and according to some among more modern sources, lunar associations as well. She is connected to land sovereignty, land fertility, bodies of water, and love.

Endnotes

17. The story, as I heard it as a child, mentions travelling 'to the far end of the world', and not around the world which could mean that the tale dates back to the time when the general belief was in a flat world. Another interpretation could be the author's reference to the boundary where human world ends and Fairy begins.

18. Lady's bedstraw (*Galium verum*) and Yellow bedstraw (*Cruciata laevipes*) are used for love magic, divination, and protection magic.

19. Summer Solstice vs Midsummer. While today we know exactly the timing for Summer Solstice, hundreds of years ago this was not entirely possible. Depending on latitude, the perception of a longest day varies. Midsummer and its celebration was therefore associated with June 23rd rather than coincide exactly to the astronomical summer solstice.

Chapter 6

Hags

Still under the fairy umbrella but different from what would be commonly called zânā, Romanian tradition mentions Muma Padurii, /Moomah Pedooree/ and Baba Cloanta /Baba Kloantzah/. These names are sometimes used in reference to the same being, but occasionally they describe two different entities or different hypostasis of the same entity. Muma Pādurii and Baba Cloanta are portrayed as very old and scary-looking women, most times acting inimically toward people. Not mentioned explicitly as a nature spirit, Muma Pādurii is yet connected with wild and remote places, and as her name suggests, with the woods, especially ancient ones.[20] She dwells in deep, uncharted forests, and her own appearance reminds one of very old, knotty, twisted trees. In stories, she appears as a hag who challenges the main protagonists, sometimes in order to test them, or with no reason other than for sport or self-serving purposes.

In the story "Fāt Frumos din Lacrimā", "Handsome Lad Born from a Teardrop", the main protagonist, Handsome Lad falls in love with a girl, possibly a fairy with night and lunar associations. The girl discloses that Muma Padurii is her mother, and warns Handsome Lad that he is in grave danger, if the hag finds him there. Because she is also in love with Handsome Lad, possibly representing a solar deity in the story, the girl reveals to him the secrets of her mother's extraordinary powers. Armed with that knowledge, Handsome Lad defeats Muma Pādurii, a possible representation of the Sun's victory over winter weather.

Baba Dochia is mentioned in connection to cold, wintry weather that occasionally hits in late spring. In one legend, Dochia is a young woman, who, one day, takes her sheep to the pasture. Allured by the nice weather, she neglectfully casts off one by one her seven cloaks. When she reaches the top, she meets twelve men gathered around a huge fire, who turn out to be the twelve months of the year.[21] Her unwise words angers the man who represents the month of April, a time when the weather is most capricious. In older versions of the legend, April's name is Prier, an archaic word that in Romanian language has the connotation of capriciousness, scarcity, and loss. April-Prier curses the girl who shortly afterwards gets lost in the mountains, while the weather deteriorates rapidly. According to the legend, Dochia ages progressively, and by the time she reaches the plateau she is an old woman barely able to walk through the raging snowstorm. Exhausted, she kneels and in the same instance turns into stone. Her flock also turns to rock. The rock formation is located in the Bucegi Mountains, in the Oriental Carpathians, and it is named Babele, meaning The Old Women. (Dobrescu, 2020)

There is an even older version of this story[22] still surviving, although not as widely circulated as the first one. In this second version, Baba Dochia is a bitter old woman who, in a fit of rage, flees up the mountain path. As she gets overheated, she drops her nine cloaks one by one. The weather gets worse with each cloak that she drops, but Dochia, in her anger, doesn't seem to care. Only when she reaches the Bucegi plateau and is caught in a sudden snow storm, does she realize her mistake. Dochia kneels, and turns into stone on the spot. In Romania, when spring weather is unusually cold, the saying goes that Baba Dochia has just dropped another one of her cloaks. These legends speak of Baba Dochia as a power that shaped the landscape and can influence weather. It is entirely possible that the legend of Baba Dochia is rooted in an older myth of a more ancient weather and land goddess, who has been gradually relegated to the ranks of fairies who bring winter weather, and in the end downgraded to a simple woman, who has a misadventure in a snowstorm.

An Cailleach, the Irish hag, is a close parallel to the

aforementioned Baba Cloantza and Baba Dochia. She is portrayed as an old woman, and in older tales she has gigantic proportions and great powers. Stories tell about Cailleach shaping the land. In one such tale Cailleach fights against giants. She pelts the giants with large masses of rock and lumps of earth which she dislodges from the ground. The place where she dug up her projectiles became Lough Arrow, in County Sligo, Ireland. Another legend talks about Cailleac Beara (one of the names used in Ireland for An Cailleach) jumping from the peak of a hill to another and dropping boulders from her apron. She had made several heaps of rocks on the hills at Loughcrew, and asked to be buried into one of them. At Loughcrew there is a large stone shaped as a chair which is known as "the hag's chair." (The School Collection Vol. 0998, p387)

An Cailleach appears to people[23]. A story mentions her supplying butter to:

King Boriche who pastured his sheep on the Mourne Mountains...This Cailleach is also alleged to have supplied butter to Leenfada when he was carrying stones for the cairn at Loughinba... [County Cavan, Ireland] ... (The School Collection Vol.0137B, p16)

Some tales speak of the Cailleach as a witch, or as having associations with witchcraft.

Long ago a Cailleach Feasog or when correctly pronounced a Cailleach Fiosach lived in this field. The Cailleach was skilled in magic. She used to cure beasts with herbs and plants. The Cailleach had a daughter who was not nearly as keen as her mother. After Nuada Fionn's (Cailleach) death there were two thousand pounds found in the house. This money which was obtained by witchcraft was given to her daughter... When this cousin of the Cailleach's went up to the kitchen to warm milk at night for her children she saw little fairies sitting in the ashes. (The Schools' Collection, Volume 0942, Page 224)

In reference to the Cailleach, Professor Daithi O'hOgain states that "In origin she was undoubtedly one of the Goddesses, or special manifestations of the Land Goddess." In the case of the Cailleach, we witness, once again, the shift from land goddess, to fairy being, to witch, occurring with the passing of time and the changing religious landscape.

Endnotes

20. Muma Pādurii translates as the Mother of the Forest. Muma is an old form for mother, *mama,* in Romanian.
21. Either the story came into existence at the time the Roman calendar was introduced, or it is a much older story adapted to fit the twelve months' calendar introduced by the Romans in 102 CE.
22. First time I heard this story told by my grandmother, Maria Mârza, in the early 1970s.
23. In this context, I am assigning An Cailleach to fairy beings.

Chapter 7

Fairies and the Dead Crossover

Both Irish and Romanian folklore and fairy lore clearly reference the connection between fairies and the deceased. In regard to the origin of fairies, one theory speaks of the Aes Sí, the People of the Mounds or the Irish fairies, as originating from among the dead. The theory finds some support in the fact that the ancient burial mounds are identified as belonging to fairies. Another supportive argument is the fact that people who were abducted or otherwise made it into the fairy mounds met there with dead people from the local community or deceased family members. However, it is more plausible to assume that while some of the dead people end up among fairies, not all the fairies are provenient from among the dead. According to Dr. Jenny Butler:

> There are traditional beliefs that deceased humans can join the fairy realm, though it is not clear whether they do so as human spirits or whether they become some other kind of entity after death. (Young, Houlbrook, 2018)

In the "Latoon Dead Hunt" story, we are told about a man who is taken to ride along the fairy procession known as the Wild Hunt. Dropped thirty miles away from the departure point, the man goes straight to the priest as soon as he makes his way back home. In telling the priest about his scary adventure the man mentions about the fairy riders who he recognized. "And he named all the gentry[24]. They were dead, all of 'em." Later in the story, the association between the fairies riding in the Wild Hunt and the dead is made stronger, in a sinister way. During the visit, the priest cautions the man against passing through the spot where he met the Hunt after dark. The man ignores the warning and, one year later, on the same day, he is found dead in the exact same location. (Lenihan, 2003)

It is not uncommon for those who end up visiting the Fairy Otherworld, to encounter ancestors or deceased relatives there. One among many such tales is "A Transaction with the Other Crowd". A man named Brian sells his horse to a fairy. Brian follows the fairy into an underground passage which leads to a luxurious mansion. The fairy pays the man the amount they agreed upon, then invites Brian to stay for dinner. Brian is inclined to accept, when a woman sneaks into the dining hall and whispers in his ear to leave the food untouched, if he ever wants to see his family again. Brian follows the woman's advice. Chased by furious fairy men, Brian escapes with the help of the woman he encountered, who, in the end, tells him that it is an aunt of his trapped in Fairy long ago. (Lenihan, 2003)

Along the lines of crossover with the dead, pondering over the role of An Dagda, who also bears the name of Don/Dunn, may bring more light on this aspect of fairy origin and relation to humans. Don or Dunn suggests a connection to the Teach Don, the House of Dead. Dunn, translating as black or dark could present An Dagda as a chthonic deity[25] and connect him with the dead. (Daimler, 2018) As mentioned previously, An Dagda is also regarded as the Fairy King of Ireland, so I am tempted to expand his attributes and abilities to that of a fairy king who also oversees, at least to some extent, the world of the dead.

In Romania, the connection between fairies and the dead is made clear on at least one occasion. The feast of the dark and powerful Rusalii is also a time to commemorate the dead. The Rusalii take their name from the Latin *rosa,* meaning rose. On the feast of Rusalii, roses are taken to graveyards to decorate the graves of the loved ones. Also, offerings of food and drink are made to the dead on this occasion, when the Rusalii themselves are celebrated in specific rituals. The connection between fairies and the dead is implied in the offerings of food and flowers on this holiday that is dedicated to both. Most of the lore that would have provided more explanations about this connection has been lost because of Christianization at first, and then because of the policy of spiritual annihilation imposed by the Communist regime.

In the lore of the Balkan area, including Romania, there is widespread belief that people who died from unnatural death, or those unbaptized, become demonic type of fairies who bring storms and hail. Also, these will roam around between Christmas and the Twelfth Day, (Pócs, 1989) which reminds of the Slua Sí or the Wild Hunt.

The Romanian Rusalii for example, sometimes sing like girls, sometimes like the dead'. (Muselea-Bârlea, 1970, Pócs, 1989)

Endnotes
24. Euphemism used for fairies in Ireland.
25. In the lore, An Dagda is featured as both god and king of fairies in Ireland.

Chapter 8

The Slua Sí, the Wild Hunt, and the Sântoaderi

Slua Sí, the Fairy Host, is a term referring to groups of fairies traveling through the air and whose presence is signaled by whirlwinds. Sometimes, the dead are believed to be part of this group, underlining once again the connection between fairies and the dead in Irish lore. The Fairy Host is known to kidnap people, hurt them physically, or drive them mad.

In her book, "A New Dictionary of Fairies", Morgan Daimler defines the Wild Hunt as "a collection of spirits – some say ghosts, or fairies – that travel through the air in storms led by a Huntsman." The hunters usually wear dark clothes, ride dark horses, and are always accompanied by dark hounds, but there are a few accounts of gray or white horses and hounds in the Wild Hunt. While they can pass unseen, their presence is betrayed by the sound of squeaking tack, jingling trappings, sound of hoofs, sound of a hunting horn, and dogs barking – all the background noise that would foretell the approaching of a hunting party. (Daimler, 2020) The Wild Hunt is connected to both fairies and the dead, and it is another example illustrating the crossover between the two. The lines between the Fairy Host and the Wild Hunt are blurry, and in many circumstances, it is hard to tell them apart.

The Wild Hunt is most active from November to the end of December, but it may appear at other times of the year as well. Both Fairy Host and Wild Hunt ride in search of humans to kidnap, sometimes returning them and sometimes not. They may occasionally ask a mortal to ride alongside them. When it doesn't end in tragedy for the human joining the hunt, the adventure may actually bring about rewards. Such is the case of the man who rides with the Fairy Host all the way to Spain and back. His family and friends would not believe him at first, but the fancy suit of Spanish clothes the Fairy Host got for the man convinces them. (Lenihan, 2003)

Another story collected is that of a man who willingly joins the Fairy Host for a nighttime ride. He notices a girl, who the fairies have kidnapped. Uttering a blessing when about to jump over a river, the man and the girl find themselves alone by the water. The girl is mute, but the man spies on the fairies who abducted her and finds out the remedy. After restoring her speech, the man takes the girl back to her family, who believed her dead. When they open the grave and the coffin, they find a block of wood instead. This story touches on multiple aspects: the Fairy Host/Wild Hunt kidnapping a human, the family holding a burial unaware that the person they believe dead has been replaced with a decoy, the human joining the ride willingly, and finding out how to undo fairy magic. The connection between fairies and the dead is evident.

While there are ways to avert abduction by the fairies, or to rescue a person on the brink of abduction, the best way to protect oneself against the Wild Hunt is to move indoors at the slightest sign of their approaching.

In Romania, Sântoaderi appear as centaur-like beings or men wearing black and riding black horses heavily shod with iron. They travel through the air, but also on the ground. Around their holiday, the Sântoaderi roam around at nighttime, and encounters with them can be lethal. They allegedly kidnap people and force them to ride along. Sometimes the kidnapped people return carrying gifts. Some other times the abducted one's return, but have either become insane or pine and die. (Kligman, 1981). Sântoaderi are active only around their homologous feast. This is a time when people stay indoors after dark and keep away from windows upon hearing the sound of iron hitting the road. Like the horses they ride, the

Sântoaderi wear shoes which are also shod with iron. It could be understood from this description that iron is not apotropaic in the case of Sântoaderi. Nowadays, the Sântoader holiday is celebrated as the feast of Saint Toader or Sântoader, three weeks before the Christian Orthodox Easter. This is also a feast of the dead, a day when food and new tableware are given freely as offerings to the departed ancestors. (Talos, 2002; Kligman, 1981) While the Church emphasizes the celebration of the saint, for many people, especially those living in rural areas, magic and harvesting herbs on the morning of Sântoader are the most important practices. It is still customary for young girls to do love magic and divination on this day. Sântoaderi resemble the Rusalii in that, albeit being dangerous, their help is very much sought after on specific occasions. A related practice, nearly extinct, involves girls of marriageable age. These girls would stay up late on the eve of Sântoader, and accompanied by older males in the family go on a nearby hilltop where they call for Sântoaderi to gift them beautiful hair and make them look most attractive. (Kligman, 1981) Such help was vital in a historical time when marriage was critically important for a woman's social status.

A widespread custom is that of clipping children's hair, especially girls' hair[26], and for animals, especially horses and cows. It is usually the older woman in the family who does the clipping, and as she does it, she asks Sântoaderi to make the hair grow beautiful and vigorous as the manes of his magical horses.

The relationship between people and these fairy beings is a paradox: Sântoaderi are extremely dangerous if encountered randomly, and women in particular are supposed to avoid them. Yet, in a certain context, they are the ones who make young girls attractive and thus more likely to find a spouse. Men emulate Sântoaderi wild nature by banding together on the night of Sântoaderi to make mischief. Like most of the fairies portrayed in both Romanian and Irish lore, Sântoaderi, despite being very dangerous, they also reward generously those brave enough to stand in their presence and approach them with due respect.

Endnotes

26. My own grandmother would clip my hair each year on the morning of Sântoader.

Chapter 9

Fairies and Animals

In the lore, animals relate to the Fairy realm in more than just one way. Stories mention domestic animals taken into Fairy, abducted or voluntarily given to the fey, animals that fairies themselves shift into, and those known as fairy animals per se. While parallels can be drawn between Irish and Romanian lore regarding fairies and animals, each among these various aspects is given different weight. For example, in Irish lore the predatory aspect of some shape-shifting fairies is strongly supported by accounts, while in Romanian lore, the stories where fairy animals partner up with humans and give assistance in times of need are most commonly encountered.

Irish lore abounds in examples of animals that fairies borrow, steal, or occasionally take with owner's consent. In Ireland fairies are fond of sneaking into barns and take out horses to ride throughout the night. Several accounts, collected from primary or secondary sources, mention horses left in stables at night, only to be found in the morning exhausted, sweaty, and with their mane's tangles. Finding a horse's mane tangled for no obvious reason is in Ireland a sure sign of fairy mischief. Even today, once rational explanations are ruled out, fairy involvement is still considered a very plausible cause for horses' exhaustion. (Lenihan, 2003)

In Ireland fairies are known to also interfere with other farm animals besides horses. Fairies are reputed for stealing cow's milk. When a cow known for her abundant milk supply runs dry, and physiological causes have been ruled out, fairies are the primary suspect. There are also accounts of fairy cows helping communities survive. Everyone benefits, until some narrow-minded person offends the cow at which point all the favors are lost.

Years ago in the famine days a fairy cow appeared near Castleisland. This cow was very valuable to the poor because she would fill a barrel or any other vessel according to the need of the household. One day an evil minded woman went to milk this cow; she took with her a strainer because she said she would carry a vessel that the cow would not fill. When she sat under the cow to milk her she disappeared and the place is now known as "Kill cow." (The School Collection, duchas.ie [27])

Fairies are also known to ride cows, and sometimes fairy cows end up among farm animals in people's households. Red cows particularly are believed to be fairy cows mingling with non-fairy cattle. When red cows have white ears, it is considered a sure sign of fairies' presence, and the white ears explained as the place where the fairy holds onto the animal while riding. It is oftentimes believed that a cow who died unexpectedly was actually taken into Fairy.

Irish lore also mentions situations where fairies would acquire an animal in a consensual way by asking to borrow or buy. A very well-known tale in Ireland talks about a boy who, while taking the cow to pasture, meets a fairy who asks to borrow the cow for one year. The fairy promises a reward in exchange. The boy is reluctant to hand the animal over to the fairy, and insists to talk first with his father. The father realizes that refusing the fairy's request could have dire consequences. He tells the child to take the cow to the fairy mound and hope for the best. One year and a day later, the boy and his father go back to the mound as the fairy had told them. There they found their cow with a beautiful white calf, waiting for them. From then on, as the story goes, the farmer and his family enjoyed healthy cattle and abundance.

(Lenihan, 2003)

There are accounts of fairies offering to buy animals from their owners. Such is the story of a man who, driven by poverty, has to sell a wonderful horse that he owns in order to pay the rent. On the way to the market the man encounters a fairy who offers to buy the horse for fifty gold coins, which is a very generous price. The man agrees to sell the horse, and then finds himself following the fairy first through a tunnel and then into a magnificent house. He is instructed where to leave the horse, receives his money, and is then invited to stay for dinner. The man suspects that something isn't right. Warned about the danger of eating fairy food and being trapped into Fairy forever, the man runs away. He makes it back home, and almost believes he dreamed it all until he realizes that the heavy heap of gold in his pocked was nearly puling his pants down. (Lenihan, 2003)

To protect against malevolent fairies, people in Ireland set up various protections. On the eve of Bealtaine[28], cattle are driven between fires lit up for this purpose, and their backs singed. Equal-arm crosses made from rowan twigs tied with red thread are placed above barn doors, and wreaths of rowan are hung inside barns.

Irish fairy traditions mention animals who are fairies themselves, and fairy beings who can take animal shape. The best noted among fairy animals are: fairy horses, hounds, and cats. The lore also abounds in stories about the shape-shifting, mischief-causing Pooka.

Fairies ride cross the air on fairy horses. The Fairy Ride makes itself heard and felt sometimes as fairy winds, and some other times as a hunting party. When the fairy horses are visible to the human eye, they appear unusually large, black or grey, with reds eyes glowing like ambers.

We mentioned the water horse, Each Uische, as an example of fairy beings connected to a certain natural environment, with bodies of water in this case. Worth reminding that the Irish Each Uische does not shape-shift into a human nor does it take the form of another animal. In this regard Each Uische is similar to the Romanian fairy horses, with the difference that the Irish water horse is extremely dangerous to humans, while the Romanian fairy horses usually fond, especially of their masters.

The pooka can take humanoid form. He can also shift into a smaller horse or pony, a goat, or dog. Pooka or púca is mischievous rather than outright malevolent. As a horse, it would trick people to get on its back. Once mounted, riders find out that they cannot dismount, nor control the horse's wild gallop. The ride ends with the human being tosses into a ditch or into water usually hurt but not killed.

Alongside other fairy animals, cats too feature in Irish fairy lore. There are accounts of people who witnessed fairies changing into cats, and accounts of cats as animals belonging to the realm of Fairy. In his book, "The Cats of Ireland", Séamus Mullarkey gives the account of a house in Co. Wicklow, Ireland, where painters renovating the house report seeing a black cat as big as a large dog. The owners of the house don't take them seriously at first. Soon after moving in, the woman realizes that something ominous is afoot. An eye witness sees a large black cat, followed by a three-foot tall man who turns himself into a cat. (Mullarkey, 2021).

Several accounts mention fairy cats, cat sí, who act like normal cats until for one reason or another betray themselves. Such is the tale of a woman who, on a winter night, upon seeing a black cat with two kittens standing in front of the door lets them in. The woman allows the cats to come near the fire to warm themselves, and kindly offers them a large saucer of milk. The cats drink their fill, and then fly up the chimney leaving for the woman a fistful of silver coins. (Mullarkey, 2021) It is customary in Ireland, on the night of Samhain, to leave outside a saucer of milk for the cat sí to earn its favor.

Fairy hounds, cu sí, make quite often apparitions. Senchaí Eddie Lenihan mentions his encounter with an exceptionally large black dog appearing in a field, near a fairy mound not far from the road. The same dog has been seen in the exact same location by several people, contemporaries to Lennihan, who knew about the same dog also being seen by their parents and grandparents[29]. Fairy hounds are usually large, black but also white occasionally, and sometimes displaying some anomaly. (Daimler, 2019)

Crows feature prominently in Irish lore but their connection to fairies is tedious at best. Irish mythology tells us that goddesses Mórrigan and Badb shape-shift into crows. From the same myths we also we also know that both Mórrigan and Badb are part of the Tuatha Dé Danann, who in retreating into the mounds joined the fairies and became fairies themselves. We could assume that this turn of events would place the Mórrigan and Badb among the Irish fairies. However, nowhere in the lore are these goddesses explicitly mentioned as fairy queens. Yet both of them are acknowledged as being among the Aes Sí, the People of the Fairy Mounds, since they are of the Tuatha Dé Danann. How much this convoluted connection makes crows fairy animals, is subject of debate.

In Romanian fairy lore, same as in fairy tales, shape-shifting happens voluntarily, or involuntarily, as the result of a curse. In "A Pig's Story" the fairy protagonist is cursed and changed into a pig by a malevolent hag who is offended by the fairy's refusal to marry one of her daughters. In the story "Harap Alb", the daughter or the Red Fairy King has the ability to change into a wren. She effects the change gladly, to deceive her suitors and lead them to their doom.

Romanian folklore lacks examples of fairies stealing, buying, or bargaining for cattle, but the examples of fairy animals are quite abundant. Most often encountered in the lore are magical horses, dogs, roosters, eagles, hawks, owls, and wrens.

Horses are among the best known and most loved fairy animals. Fairy men are almost always accompanied by such horses who act as advisors and protectors. Before accepting a new master, fairy horses test the character and intelligence of whoever seeks to ride them. In the homologous story, the fairy horse first presents himself to Harap Alb in the guise of a very old and sick horse, completely unsuited for the long journey awaiting the protagonist. The horse then proceeds to test Harap Alb's patience and resolve. When the testing ends, the horse magically reveals himself in all his splendor, white, winged, and able to talk. This example of fairy horse, or horse with magic abilities, is far from unique. Aside from fairy lore, Stephan the Great[30], a most prominent Romanian prince, owned a horse believed to be magic. This horse, Catalan, gets significant credit for the many victories that Stephan won.

The aforementioned Sântoaderi are a somewhat distinct type of fairy beings who are contingent to fairy horses yet not exclusively part of them. As already discussed, Sântoaderi are centaur-like beings extremely dangerous, yet also helpful in very specific circumstances. Aside from them, the lore also mentions the Sântoader's horses. An ancient deity whose name and holiday have been conflated with the homologous Saint Toader, Sântoader is known as the owner of many fairy horses. He is invoked as a protector of horses and farm animals. Depending of the region, the lore and custom emphasize more the centaur-like beings who are his companions, or the fairy horses he owns. (Ghinoiu, 2004; Talos, 2002)

Fairy dogs, albeit not always explicitly acknowledged as such, are also part of the folklore. There are no mentions of fairies shape-shifting into dogs, but dogs who allegedly belong with fairy animals. Fairy dogs are unusually large and black and appear in solitary places, oftentimes at night. Folklore also mentions demons who appear as large black dogs, and this could be one among the several examples of fairies being demonized, conflated or glossed together with demons. Several stories tell about encounters with dogs who are tasked by their Otherworldly masters to either test the mettle of human protagonists, or plainly keep them away. Fairy dogs could inform their owners about honest or dishonest intention humans hold, or take initiative in punishing or rewarding as they see fit.

In the story "The Old Man's Daughter and the Old Woman's Daughter", a fairy she-dog meets both girls when they cross the boundary into the Otherworld. The she-dog appears first to the Old Man's Daughter pretending to be wounded and in need of help. The girl does not hesitate to tear stripes of cloth form her own dress to make bandages and nurse the dog's wounds. The same she-dog, in the same pitiful state, appears to the Old Woman's Daughter and makes the same requests. The Old Woman's daughter avoids the dog altogether, indifferent to its pleas for help. Upon returning, the two girls encounter the she-dog again. The dog, now looking white and fluffy as a cloud, wears a gold collar studded with precious stones. The Old Woman's Daughter draws near the she-dog attempting to trick her and steal the collar. The dog bites this girl's fingers, then gifts the collar to the Old Man's Daughter, a very typical resolution for a story involving Romanian fairy animals, who usually reward or punish proportionally to the human's kindness or lack of it.

The fairy eagles have almost gigantic proportions, and fondness of humans it is not their default. However, they are righteous as much as they are powerful willing to go to the greatest length to repay a favor. The encounters with fairy eagles feature in many stories, and follow this exact same pattern.

The human male protagonist[31] ends up in the Otherworld and wanders around in a dangerous mountain landscape. He arrives just in time to see a gigantic snake trying to reach a nest where helpless baby-eagles cry for help. The man overcomes the snake, and the grateful little eagles advise him on how to enlist the help of mother-eagle. The little eagles warn the man that, without their protection, their mother would eat him immediately without giving him a chance to explain anything. They hide the man in their nest which as big as a hut. When their mother returns, she immediately senses the scent of the human, and asks her children to deliver him immediately. The chicks' bargain for the man's life explaining that they would be dead without his intervention. The mother-eagle promises under oath that she will not harm the human, and will help him in any way she can. At this point the chicks bring the man out from his hideaway. To the chicks' dismay, the mother-eagle swallows the man whole. Then she immediately spits him out and vows to help him on his quest. From that moment on, throughout the story, the man displays magical abilities. The swallowing and regurgitation could be understood as an initiatory ritual during which the fairy eagle transfers to the human magical powers, making him akin to fairies.

This particular episode has an equivalent in the Irish lore, where fairies attempt to turn a human child into one of their own. A boy is kidnapped by fairies who wash him in an attempt to erase any imprint the human world had left on him. It is understood that once the cleansing is complete, the boy could be turned into a fairy through further initiatory practices. Since the child has a bramble thorn under one of his nails which the fairies cannot find, they give up and return him to the human world. The boy cannot be immersed enough into Fairy to become a fairy himself because of the tiny trace of human world that clings onto him. In the Romanian story, even after being swallowed by the fairy eagle, acquiring magical power that make him akin to fairies, the man does not change into a fairy nor does he abandon living in the human world.

The lark is another example of a fairy bird often encountered in Romanian lore. There are numerous stories where a fairy lark helps the protagonist whether the protagonists themselves are humans or fairies. The fairy lark, same as the fairy eagle, has very large proportions. Despite its intimidating size, the lark always acts friendly to the protagonists. Fairy larks usually help by showing the path to a hidden destination or even allowing the protagonist to ride on their back for fast transportation. In the aforementioned "Pig Story", by allowing the woman to ride on his back, the lark shortens the trip to only seven days. Without such help, it would have taken the woman in the story one whole year to reach her destination. Same as the episode where the fairy eagle first swallows but then aids the human, the helpful lark motif appears almost unchanged in lore across various regions of Romania.

There is no mention of the owl being a bird of Fairy in the way that eagle and lark are, but there are stories of fairies changing in to owls. Both Mihai Eminescu and Ioan Slavici, in the folklore collections they wrote and published in the nineteenth century, retell a much older tale of a fairy queen and her entourage of six fairies who shift back and forth between owl and human form.

A young prince marries a beautiful woman, and discovers that she is a fairy queen. The fairy queen moves in with her husband but also brings along her six companions. All seven fairies spend part of the day in human form and part as owls. The prince is bound by oath not to reveal anyone his wife's fairy nature and shape-shifting habits. However, the prince soon becomes discontent with the owl shape his wife takes, and breaks the vow of secrecy. Informed about the situation, the prince's mother advises her son to burn the feathers the owls shed when they turn into humans. In doing so, the prince loses his wife who shape-shifts regardless of him burning her feathers, and fly away. Same as in the "Pig's Story", the prince has to overcome innumerable obstacles to reunite with his wife, which he then gladly accepts in whatever form she takes.

Endnotes

27. The Schools' Collection, Volume 0449, Page 296 https://www.duchas.ie/en/cbes/4713225/4709263/4815309
28. The night of April 30th.
29. https://www.youtube.com/watch?v=TKl9y5VlTzQ
30. https://www.britannica.com/biography/Stephen-prince-of-Moldavia
31. Romanian fairy lore is heavily gendered.

Chapter 10

Dragons, Zmei, and Balauri

In this book I have chosen to write a separate section for dragons, because as we will see, they don't really fit alongside neither fairy animals of the kind already being discussed or fairy human-like beings. So, the Irish dragon, and the equivalent Romanian zmeu *(pl. zmei, /zmehee/)* and balaur *(pl. balauri, /bah-lAH-oo-ry/)* are in a class of their own. In both cultures dragons are known as fearsome and destructive. Whether embodying chthonic forces beyond humans' ability or other fairies' ability to control, destructive nature spirits, or featured as anti-heroes in numerous tales, dragons inspire fear and reverence.

In Irish lore, the dragon is not the ordinary villain. The dragon is a magical creature virtually impossible to defeat. The dragon can also appear as a challenger to the protagonist, since overcoming the beast is a test of intelligence and fortitude for the human who, in subduing the dragon raises in status and is initiated into a different life stage and position.

For the young Finn Mac Cumhaill, stopping Aillen of the Flaming Breath becomes his opportunity to advance and become the leader of the Fianna warrior bands. Defeating the dragon who, each year at Samhain, would burn down the royal seat at Tara, is an initiatory experience for Finn. In engaging Aillen, Finn must show determination and mastery of self in addition to physical prowess and battle skills. The dragon that Finn has to confront has gigantic proportions, and spits fire. Additionally, he uses enchantment to lull people to sleep in order to circumvent any valiant human's ability to fight. Finn learns to use a spear to keep himself awake, engages Aillen, and saves Tara and its people. One of the best-known stories in Irish myth, the story of Finn overtaking the dragon, is actually the story of Finn's coming of age and the origin of the Fianna[32].

Another dragon story from Ireland talks about Amergin waiting for the frightening creature to emerge from the Uimh na Gat, the Cave of the Cats. In her book, "Stories of Old Ireland Retold", Lora O'Brien writes an exquisitely beautiful reiteration of this myth. In the story, Amergin realizes that he needs something unprecedented to overcome the dragon, a shape-shifting creature capable of counteracting whatever form of magic Amergin would employ. Amergin outsmarts the dragon, who emerges as a fire creature, and tricks him to look at himself in a nearby body of water. He then coaxes the dragon to charge at his own reflection, and the water annihilates the fiery being. (O'Brien, 2018)

Romanian lore displays a variety of dragons. While they are all very large, fearsome looking, and dangerous, they can occasionally show benevolence toward people. There are also variations in the way various kinds of dragons look. The notorious balaur is a dragon with the aspect of a gigantic reptile, with one or several heads. Typically, balauri spit fire, spew venom, and cause destruction when hitting with their tail. Some are earth-bound, but some other have wings and can fly. Balauri are predatory beings. They raid human communities to capture people they eat, and hoard treasures which they guard fearsomely. Occasionally, a human community would benefit from the protection of a balaur who can dump hail or raise storms to affect another rival human community. (Pócs, 2018)

Zmei are dragons who share their predatory nature and enormous size with their cousins, the balauri. Differently from balauri, most zmei have human bodies. They have animal heads, usually wolf-like, and sometimes reptilian features such as thick skin with scales. Some zmei have only one head, but others have as many as three. Zmei kidnap women whom they wish to marry. Zmei display physical strength, and magical abilities, which makes them hard to overcome. While there is no gender differentiation for balauri, the zmei are gendered. The figure of a zmeu-father is conspicuously absent. Muma Zmeilor, the Mother of Zmei, is an authority figure who features in many stories. The name is generic, but the actual character is not. In each tale where she appears, Muma Zmeilor is the mother of one or several zmei, but she is never intended as the mother of all zmei.

In her work, Dr. Èva Pócs mentions zmei who have shared some characteristics of balauri – such as having wings, looking partly reptilian – and who can influence weather. These zmei can bring hail and destructive thunderstorms, and for this reason human communities ward against zmei and try to appease them with offerings. Warding and negotiating with zmei is the purview on the fairy witch, known in Romanian tradition as Soimancā, doftoroaie, or plainly vrājitoare /vruh-zee-toah- re/ meaning witch. (Pócs, 2018)

Endnotes

32. Fianna were small, partly independent warrior bands composed of youth, some aristocratic, who did not reach yet the legal age to inherit land. These warrior bands would serve the community by offering protection. (https://irishimbasbooks.com)

Chapter 11

Protection

Since it is difficult to understand what moves fairies to act the way they do, both Romanian and Irish fairy lore advocate for caution. The basic and most widespread approach consists in making offerings and keeping out of their way. There are also additional safety measures to keep malevolent fairies away, some of them common to both Ireland and Romania and some others specific to each culture.

It shall be mentioned that in Romania many among zâne are not hostile to humans, and when approached respectfully they can turn into powerful and reliable allies. These zâne enjoy their offerings placed by special trees known to be theirs. Such trees are usually solitary ones, but zâne usually claim the most beautiful tree specimen among the trees of a glove or glen. Since such zâne don't pose a threat unless disturbed or offended, Romanians don't worry about setting up protections against them. However, the benevolent zâne are only one part among the fairy population in Romania, and quite little can be done to protect against the less benevolent ones. For example, there is next to nothing that can protect against Muma Pădurii, Baba Cloanta, other than putting as much distance as possible between oneself and her. Fire is said to offer some protection against Muma Pădurii, despite that in many tales she is specifically described as keeping a fire lit in her own house. In this specific situation, iron works apotropaic to defend newborns, but it isn't clear whether it protects people once they move past childhood. Also, iron, the most widespread recommended defense against the Irish fairies, does not work against neither Iele nor Sântoaderi, the most dangerous among the Romanian fairies. Horse shoes are somewhat of an exception to this rule, but most likely, it is their association with horses that confer protective qualities, rather than the iron used in the crafting of the horseshoe.

Iele, the fairies who are decidedly not fond of humans, are deterred by horse skulls. Horse heads are carved as decorations on door jambs, gates, or on posts planted in the yard. Long ago, in some areas of the country it was customary to have an actual horse skull on a post in one's yard as protection against the Iele. (Kligman, 1981)

Mugwort is known to break fairy magic and keep malevolent fairies away, including the Iele. In Romania, basil is also used for protection against all kinds of fairy attacks and fairy-induced illnesses. Romanian fairy lore mentions people who have fairy guardians and fairy allies gifting them basil or other herbs to use for personal protection and healing work. This is similar to those among the Irish fairy witches or fairy doctors who gain their knowledge of herbs and healing directly from fairies. Saint John's Wort and rowan wood are used for protection in Ireland, but not in Romania. Christian symbols such as crossing oneself, specific prayers, and holy water, are used in both Ireland and Romania to protect against fairies with various degrees of success.

Chapter 12

Other Forms of Fairy–Human Interaction

According to Romanian tradition, ignoring the warnings from fairies guarding certain places never ends well for trespassers. As illustrated by the story of the tree cutters, which was discussed earlier, those who act driven by greed and treat fairy guardians with disrespect, could pay with their lives. The fear of fairies kept many mounds[33], cairns[34], and tree specimens safe for hundreds of years, and it still does so today. Irish lore records many examples of people hit by bad luck after disturbing fairy forts or fairy trees.

A story recorded by Eddie Lenihan tells the tale of three men who had fairy forts on their properties. The man telling the story mentioned his respect and fear he felt about fairies and his resolution to leave the mound on his property untouched. The second man said he planned on cutting down the trees and bushes on the right side of the mound on his property without disturbing the mound itself, while the third man scoffs at the other two and brags that he'd tear down the mound and "make the fairies homeless." (Lenihan, 2003) The person telling the story continues the account by stating that one week later, both men who disturbed fairies' property were dead. The man who bulldozed down the fairy fort died, crushed under a shed that collapsed on top of him. On the same day, the man who cut the trees on one side of the fort died in his sleep. The man who treated the fairies' property with respect lived to tell the tale, literally.

Fairy encounters may have happy resolutions for those among humans who show respect and generosity. A very well-known tale in Ireland is that of a poor peasant woman who receives an unexpected visit from a beggar. The beggar, also a woman, asks for a little bit of food saying that she is starving.

The peasant woman explains that there is only a little bit of flour left in the chest, but she would gladly give half of it to her guest. The beggar takes the flower and tells the woman that she will never lack flour in her chest from that moment on. The woman realized that she was visited by a fairy, her belief finding validation in the course of the following days when no matter how much flour she used, there was always enough left in her chest. (Evans-Wenz, 1911)

Similar examples are found in Romanian folklore. In the popular story "Fata babei si fata mosului", "The Daughter of the Old Woman, and the Daughter of the Old Man," two young women, stepsisters, encounter Muma Pădurii, The Old Mother of the Wood. The encounter has a different outcome for each girl since they handle things very differently. The old man's daughter takes seriously the various assignments that Muma Padurii asks her to complete. She goes out of her way to clean and cook for Muma Pădurii, who has almost unreasonable standards set up for any task, no matter how trivial. The girl treats kindly, and washes and feeds the snakes, dragons, and other similar beings that Muma Padurii has for pets, and seeks earnestly to help without targeting any special reward or favor. Pleased with her service, Muma Padurii asks the girl to go in the attic and pick up her reward. The girl finds many chests laying around, some studded with precious stones, some gilded in gold, some plain and ordinary looking. The old man's daughter picks up the most unassuming chest she could find. In contrast, the old woman's daughter acts very disrespectful and conceited. She rushes through her tasks, the same ones assigned to her step-sister, hurts Muma Padurii's beloved pets, and promptly demands to be rewarded for her efforts. Once in the attic, she picks up the largest, most ornamented chest she could find. Muma Padurii instructs the girls to only open their chest when arriving home. Upon doing so, the old man's daughter finds her chest to be a bottomless pit of gold coins, jewelry, and the finest cattle. The old woman's daughter instead is strangled by two giant serpents, who come out of the chest, once she opens it. (Ispirescu, 2016, Stancescu, 1892)

Both Irish and Romanian fairy lore contain examples of marriages between human and fairy partners. There is a common element to these stories, namely, the fairy partner demands secrecy from their human spouse. In the majority of cases, the human partner breaks the promise and reveals to family or friends that they are married to a fairy. There are heavy consequences, and the chance to remediate is very rare, if present at all.

The Romanian tale, "Povestea Porcului", "The Pigs Story", is a popular example. An old man and his wife rescue a piglet stuck in the mud. Being childless and becoming affectionate to the piglet, they adopt it as their child. It turns out that the piglet has magical powers. He builds a golden bridge for the emperor, who faithful to a promise he made, gives his daughter in marriage to the one who could accomplish such a feat – in this case, the piglet. Each night the piglet sheds his skin and turns into a most handsome young man. He advises his wife not to tell anyone about this change. The girl doesn't keep the secret and her fairy husband is bound to leave her despite mutual love and expecting a child. Through making friends with two fairy queens – named Saint Friday and Saint Sunday in the story, and overcoming many adversities, the woman is reunited with her husband.

In Irish lore, the story "The Debility of the Ulstermen" is one example of a human-fairy relationship that ends badly, in this case for the fairy partner. As the story has it, one day Macha, woman of the Fairy, comes out of a fairy mound and walks into the house of a noble, handsome, and rich widower. She becomes his wife, and he continues to prosper. Macha warns her husband not to speak about her to anyone: "… for our union will continue only if thou dost not speak of me in the assembly." (maryjones.us) Despite his promise of not mentioning his wife to anyone, Crunnchu, the husband, fails to keep his word and, at a fair, brags about his wife's ability to outrun the king's horses. Insulted by Crunnchu's claim, the king orders Macha to be brought in to race against his horses, and in case she refuses or fails, her husband shall be put to death. On the brink of giving birth, Macha finds no clemency, and is forced to race to save her husband. She wins the race, gives birth to twins, and curses the Ulstermen who treated her with cruelty and disrespect to be afflicted by labor-like pains in the hour of their direst need. The story doesn't mention what exactly Macha does after this. Maybe she just returns into the sí mound. However, the relationship ends there.

Some fairies act as regional guardians. According to the lore, certain communities or areas in Romania are under the protection of specific fairies. Each among such fairies, cares for its own community and will go as far as stealing the food supplies from other neighboring communities to support theirs. Oftentimes, this brings fairy guardians at war with each other: those trying to steal supplies and those trying to defend them. Guardian fairies also fight against fairies commanding storms, hail, and destructive winds to protect humans from impending natural disasters. (Pòcs, 1989)

In Irish lore, different fairy queens have guardianship of different areas. (O'Brien, 2021) Some among the fairy guardians of places are:

- Áine is connected to Lough Gur, in County Limerick, and Dun Áine, in County Louth.
- Aoibheal is connected with Carraig Liath, in County Clare.
- Cliodhna is associated with Carraig Cliodhna, in Cork.
- Úna, Oona, or Unagh, is said to live with her husband, fairy king Finnbheara, Knockmaa, or at her own residence in County Tipperary.

In the Irish tradition, the ban sidhe is a fairy woman connected to a certain family, and who fulfills the role of announcing the impending death of a person in that family. The connection between ban sidhe and one specific family goes on for generations. Some among the fairy queens are also known to accomplish the role of ban sidhe. Cliodhna, the queen of the Munster fairies, is connected to the families McCarthy and O'Keefe, acts as banshee[35], and some sources mention her as queen of all banshees. (Daimler, 2019)

In Ireland and Romania alike, fairies are known for their self-serving agendas. In Ireland, they kidnap musicians and poets to entertain audiences during fairy parties, abduct young women and men for breeding stock, borrow women who just gave birth to nurse fairy babies, and steal babies and young children to swell their own numbers. (Evans-Wentz, 1911, Lady Wilde 1826/1991) Stolen people are replaced with decoys that are enchanted to look identically to the ones taken away. Sick fairy babies or old fairies are substituted to the human babies abducted; such substitutes are known in Ireland as changelings. The lore mentions various remedies to compel the fairies to take away the changeling and return the stolen child. Some methods are benign, such as tricking the changeling to react or behave in a way that betrays their age. Some other methods range from mild, such as threatening the changeling with fire, to outright torture. (Lady Wilde, 1826/1991).

In Romania, fairies abduct musicians and poets, who they occasionally return, and occasionally abduct babies and children. Among the fairies populating the Romanian landscape, Muma Pādurii is the best known for stealing young children (http://mythologica.ro). Some fairy queens find ways to convince, or trick families into handing over their newborns, such as in the story of the "White Kitten" collected by Nestor Urechia, and published together with other tales about fairies in "Zânele din Valea Cerbului". Romanian lore also mentions changelings, but it is not a widespread phenomenon, at least not as widespread as in the Irish lore. Sometimes substitutes are left in place of the stolen babies, and sometimes not. When a family suspects that their child has been replaced with a changeling, a fire is lit and the suspected changeling is threatened to be thrown in. If the suspect cries like a human child, this is considered proof of a regular baby. If the suspect is a changeling, the fire threat would make them give away their true identity. Most stolen children are never seen again. Very rarely, a child given away under constrain or through trickery would reunite with their birth family. (Urechia, 1904)

Both Irish and Romanian sources mention fairies' involvement with people's destiny. According to the Irish lore, a good deed toward a fairy could result in the fairy bestowing blessings on the new mother and her baby. These blessings could be in the form of protection against other malicious fairies or a special gift that brings luck and prosperity to the baby later in life. (Evans-Wentz, 1911, Lenihan, 2003)

Romanian tales mention fairies who show up when children in certain families are born to make gifts and prophecies about these children's future. The theme of fairy gifts bestowed upon children at birth has been spun into more recent folklore and fairy tales in very interesting ways. Fairies may strip children of kindness or intelligence for example, leaving them to face the quest of regaining what was taken away from them. (Urechia, 1904) Another theme that has been incorporated into modern lore, is that a fairy intervention in a human's destiny is directly connected to a fairy's personal interest. One such example is the story "Cele Doua Fete de Morar", "The Miller's Two Daughters": a fairy queen weaves the fate of two young people bringing them together because the series of actions involved in the process of connecting them, leads to the dispelling of a curse laid on the fairy queen by her rival. Albeit the story itself is bordering on folkloresque, its core idea remains true to older fairy lore that mention fairy acting based on self-serving interests and not from just a natural fondness toward humans.

Endnotes

33. In Ireland, mounds of earth covering Bronze Age structures that were seen as places where fairies dwell or use as gateways between their world and the world of humans.
34. Neolithic and Bronze Age burial and or ceremonial structures in Ireland made of stones stacked up, sometimes enclosing inner chambers, sometimes not.
35. Anglicized form of ban sidhe.

Chapter 13

Tir Na nÓg and "Youth without Aging, and Life without Death"

A theme with archaic origins represented in both Irish and Romanian fairy lore is that of a land where inhabitants are exempt from aging. From studying different sources portraying fairies, one may conclude that they are believed to be either as immortal or as having an extremely long lifespan. Fairy, the otherworldly place inhabited by fairies, or at least parts of it, may thus be places where young age is eternal.

Oldest recorded Irish story, Echtra Condla[36], features a fairy encounter that occurs between Connla, son of king Conn the Hundred-Fighter, and a woman of the fey. While walking with his father on the Hill of Uisneach, Connla saw a woman peculiar in her appearance.

Said Connla, "Where do you come from, woman?" The woman answered:
"I come from the Lands of the where there is neither death, nor want, nor sin. We keep feast without need for service. Peace reigns among us strife. A great fairy-mound (*sid*) it is, in which we live; we are called 'folk of the fairy-mound' (*aes side*)." (Mary Jones, The Celtic Literature Collective)

The fairy woman thus describes a land where there is no death, the concept of sin is absent, and nobody lacks anything. The inhabitants of the island always feast but never have to work, and there's always peace. Such places of eternal life and perpetual abundance are a typical description of an otherworldly place where many mortals long to go.

In another story, Oisin, the son of Fionn Mac Cuill goes

to Fairy. After what he perceived as a span of three years, Oisin is seized by a strong desire to see his land and his own people. Despite being warned against traveling back home, Oisin leaves. His fairy wife gives him a horse, and urges him to never dismount. While traveling through the world of humans Oisin realizes that hundreds of years have passed. He accidentally gets off the horse, and as soon as he touches the ground, time catches up with him. Oisin dies and turns into dust. The theme of time working differently in such places of eternal youth and never-ending abundance is present in both Irish and Romanian lore.

The Romanian tale "Youth without Aging, and Life without Death", "Tinerete fără Bātrânete si Viatā fārā de Moarte", speaks of a prince's quest to reach the Land of Eternal Youth, where everyone stays young forever, and death never reaches them. The prince leaves his aggrieved parents, and wanders the world in search of the magical land of eternal youth. After several years, he reaches a valley enveloped in thick mists, and after crossing through, he comes upon a palace inhabited by three fairies. They gladly take the prince to live with them, and tell him that "he may go everywhere he chooses; but one place he must never enter, and if he did, he would fare very badly indeed. The place was a small valley, and it was called the Valley of Tears." (Ispirescu, 2016) One day, while hunting, the prince unwittingly trespasses into the Valley of Tears. Suddenly, a longing to see his parents and his birthplace seizes him. The longing becomes torturous, and despite the fairies and his magical horse begging him to stay, he decides to leave. As he travels, he discovers that what seemed to be days and months in the fairies' castle, was hundreds of years in the world of humans. The prince ages rapidly while browsing through the ruins of the palace where he was born. Barely standing, he goes into the cellar where he finds a long-forgotten chest. Upon opening the chest, Death comes out of it and slaps the prince who crumbles to dust.

Endnotes

36. The Adventures of Connla the Fair https://www.maryjones. us/ctexts/connla.html

Chapter 14

Irish Fairy Doctors and Romanian Medicine Women

In her article "The Witch, the Bean Feasa, and the Fairy Doctor in Irish Culture" Morgan Daimler explains the connection between certain Irish practitioners of folk medicine and fairies.

In modern American terms we tend to call anyone who works with low magic or folk magic a witch; however, from an Irish perspective such people actually fell into roughly three groups: witches called caillí (singular cailleach) in Irish, fairy doctors, and mná feasa (singular ban feasa). It is important to note up front that all three of these terms can be and sometimes are used interchangeably, and a single person may be given all three labels by different people. (Daimler, 2014)

To this day, in Ireland, the usual recommendation is to stay away from fairies, and if you can't stay away, then stay on their good side. In practical terms, this means leaving out offerings for Na Daoine Maithe, and not touching anything that belongs to them. However, there is a history of people who maintained partnerships with fairies. Such people were chosen by the fairies themselves, on criteria that are not entirely clear. They would become skilled in healing and sometimes prophecy. The roles of a fairy doctor and that of a bean feasa who are mentioned in the paragraph above, overlapped in some aspects. They are both known to have obtained their knowledge, entirely or at least in part, from fairies. The bean feasa, which translates as wise woman, is called to solve all kinds of problems: retrieve a lost or stolen object, effect a cure for a common disease or injury, apply protective magic to home, its inhabitants, and the cattle, avert attacks from malevolent witches, and similar endeavors. The fairy witch was specifically called when fairy involvement was suspected, but this is not to be taken in a rigid sense. Typically, the bean feasa does not teach what she knows to anyone. The Fairy doctor teaches others, and passes down her knowledge to family members, most commonly to her own children or grandchildren. (Wilde, 1991, Daimler, 2014)

Biddy Early from County Clare is, beyond any shade of a doubt, the best-known fairy doctor in Ireland. She was reputed for her blue bottle, a gift from fairies, that she consulted to provide advice and cures to those seeking her help. (https://www.clarelibrary.ie) The life of Biddy Early and the numerous stories circulating about her make up a large body of literature. According to several sources, local priests tried to silence Biddy and dissuade people from seeking her help. Their effort was to no avail. However, the end of her life finds Biddy Early "Rosary in hands...." (Rogers, 2016) After administering her the final rites, the priest then throws the famous blue bottle into the nearby lake. Many attempts were made to drag the lake to find the bottle without success. The ruins of Biddy Early's house are still standing, and her story is as alive today as it ever was.

While the best known, Biddy Early is not the only known fairy doctor in Ireland. Cork prides itself with Máire Ní Mhurchú, who was known to travel with fairies and have knowledge of events happening elsewhere. Eibhlin Ní Ghuinníola from Kerry County had a fairy lover who accompanied her whenever she went to gather herbs, and who supposedly taught her about herbal medicine. (O'Crualaoich, 2006).

Many Romanian and Irish fairy medicine people[37] alike claim unequivocally to have gotten their skills and knowledge from the fairies themselves. The Romanian tradition of people working in partnership with fairies only survives in trace forms, and nominal records of actual practitioners are lost. Unfortunately, no name of fame or notoriety from the past made it into records, and today those who still have such connections with fairies are few and far between. Anthropologist Dr. Maria Vivod, had the chance to witness an event extremely rare to come by: a ritual performed by an actual fairy seer. Dr. Vivod investigated the practice of working with fairies in a Romanian-speaking community living in nowadays Serbia[38]. In her documentary, Dr. Vivod describes her interaction with contemporary fairy seers who proudly claim to be carriers of an ancient tradition. The term 'fairy seer' was created impromptu by Dr. Vivod, because the native name used for the Vlah women who work with fairies, Soimance, is not translatable. The fairy seer interviewed, Ivanka, allowed Dr. Vivod to assist in the entire ritual, the dance, the chanting, and the trance state. Ivanka told her story and also mentioned by name her fairy allies, Sânziana, Diana, and Maica Precista (Great Mother). She spoke about the people who become fairy seers. In the Vlah community, it is believed that the seventh child in a family possesses the gift of seeing fairies and may be called to work with them. Also, in some people emotional or physical trauma or illness can act as a catalyst for the initiatory experience. However, Ivanka the fairy seer, states that "anyone who wants to see the creatures can, it is only a matter of will". (Vivod, 2018) Those who choose to pursue the path of a fairy seer undergo an initiatory rite, which involves ecstatic trance, climbing up a mountain top, or climbing up a tree, most often a pear tree.

Once initiated, the people chosen by fairies have to comply with their demands. The fairy seers are tasked to travel via a trance state or physically with the fairies, who teach them about healing, prophecy, and magic. Noncompliance leads to corporal punishment. Ivanka herself woke up with bruises on her arms and with her legs numb on one occasion when she did not obey the requests that fairies had for her. According to Ivanca and another healer from the community, Mila, the fairies are very nice and generous to those who are in service to them and who fulfill their duties as the fairies expect. (Vivod, 2018)

I grew up with my grandmother, a medicine woman or doftoroaie[39], who could see and communicate with fairies. In this regard, she was similar to the Irish fairy doctors, and an almost identical match to the fairy seers interviewed by Dr. Vivod. My grandmother, Maria, was not an isolated case albeit a rare one. Herself, and the few among other practitioners of folk medicine that I encountered, received knowledge and skills from otherworldly beings whom they identified as zâne, or fairies. Similar to other practitioners within the culture, my grandmother kept a low profile about her fairy connections, and the name of her fairy collaborators secret.

One of the main jobs of a doftoroaie was, and still is, to foil attempts made by Muma Padurii to steal babies or young children. A doftoroaie is also asked to intervene in case of fairy-induced illnesses. To protect a baby or a young child against abduction or harm caused by inimical fairies, the doftoroaie would have the child and their mother undergo a specific ritual. At sunrise or sunset, the doftoroaie places herself on the threshold facing outside. The mother holding the child in her arms stands behind doftoroaie with her back toward the door. The doftoroaie spills water from a dish and threatens Muma Pădurii with drowning. "The Powers of the Water shall drown you," is the formula that I heard being used. Then she lights up a torch and waves it while threatening the malevolent fairy with burning, "The Powers of the Fire shall char you." Last, the doftoroaie takes an ax and knocks the threshold and the door jambs with it while threatening Muma Pădurii with chopping her into pieces: "Shall you approach again, this ax will chop you into tiny pieces that the Power of Wind shall blow into all four corners of the world." The doftoroaie mandates the inimical being to leave the child and their mother alone, and be smitten, drowned, burned, and scattered if they'd ever show up again.

The axe is then placed under the child's bed. The doftoroaie concludes the ritual with an invocation to the powers of Water, Fire, and Wind to protect the baby and his mother against Muma Pădurii, and makes offerings to the spirits of the place and those goodly inclined among zâne to protect the house and those living in it.

As mentioned earlier, the Rusalii are zâne, feared for their ability to cause madness, death, or to maim people. Although, typically they are not fond of humans on certain dates, the Rusalii, or at least few among them, side with the men carrying out specific ceremonies to heal and bless entire communities. The healing ceremonies take the form of a dance named Călusari /Ku-loo-SHAri/ or Călus /Ku-LOOsh/. Those engaging in this dance are known by the homonym Călusari. This dance, which is in fact a ritual of the highest level of complexity, is the expression of a particular human-fairy relationship. Călus sophisticated choreography, high speed, and numerous jumps convey the sense of flying and that of crossing the boundaries between human world and the world of Fairy. On this occasion man acquires powers similar to the fairies – flight and magic – albeit temporarily. Before proceeding, the Călusari ask for the blessings of the Fairy Queen known by the names of Irodia, Aradia, Arada, Irodiada, or Rosalia: the name can be different in different parts of Romania. The dancers assemble ceremonially and function as a brotherhood. Their grouping and functioning, including fighting with rival bands, is a not too different from the warrior bands known as the fianna in Irish myth. The Călusari act under the protection and guidance of the Fairy Queen. This is another example of paradox within fairy-human relationships: while their alleged mission is to heal the harm done by the Rusalii, fairies who are under the command of Irodiada, the Fairy Queen, it is herself protecting the ritual dancers while they are on a mission to rid their community members of the harm caused by Rusalii. The relationship between Rusalii and Cālusari is a complicated one and beyond the scope of this study. Suffice to say that the Cālusari's mission is to bring about healing, to protect the community against malevolent spirits through the energy raised in ritual dancing, and to propitiate growth and abundance. They are granted special powers in exchange for promises they made and by virtue of the oath taken upon initiation. What is said and what the Calusari promise under oath is a very well-guarded secret.

Since the moment they assemble and throughout the whole time they work together, the Cālusari carry with them mugwort or wormwood, garlic, and salt. Mugwort, wormwood, and garlic are known in Romanian folk magic as protective against Iele and dangerous spirits. Salt is known to both symbolize and attract abundance (sympathetic magic), for healing, and also for placating harmful energies. On the last day of the holiday, usually the second or third day following the feast of Rusalii, the Cālusari would, after their last ritual performance, disband. Part of the ritual is breaking of the 'flag' they carry throughout their performances. This flag, a staff made of pine or fir, has attached at its top a bundle containing mugwort or wormwood, garlic, and possible other regional herbs known for healing and apotropaic use. Shreds from the broken flag and bits of the herbs in the bundle are given out or sold to spectators. Women would also try to steal or obtain threads from the Cālusari belts which are made from wool or other different textile fibers. Women, the ones who traditionally wield the magical powers, use these threads to weave them into charms for protection against malevolent fairies and other kinds of spirits. (Kligman 1981). The dance of Cālusari is still practiced today and is regaining the ritual and magical connotations, nearly obliterated during half a century of spiritual annihilation. Like all things fairy, traditions regarding them seem to nearly vanish yet never actually disappear.

Endnotes

37. I came up with the name of fairy medicine people as an umbrella term to cover the mná feasa, fairy witches, fairy doctors of Ireland, and those people in Romanian who work in partnership with fairies.

38. Vlach/Vlah language—a daco-romanian dialect has about 100,000 speakers and is spoken by the Vlach/Vlah community of eastern Serbia, known by the endonym *limba română (Romanian language)*; more: http://lacito.vjf.cnrs.fr/ ALC/Languages/ Valaque_popup.htm (Vivod, 2015)

39. Doftoroaie was and to a lesser extent still is the name used to define practitioners of folk medicine in the area where I grew up.

Conclusion

The territory of nowadays Romania sits at the junction of western and eastern Europe thus constituting itself into a geographic bridge between Celtic speaking cultures and Slavic ones. Ireland sits far out to the west, in opposition to Romania's location on the map of Europe. Far apart enough to develop quite distinct characters, Irish and Romanian Fairy lore display a significant parallelism regarding fairy beliefs and people's experiences with fairies. These oftentimes striking similarities are regarded as "Indo-European (Pócs, 1989) and Celtic heritage remains which are common to both cultures" (Pòcs 1989; Campbell 1900; id. 1902; O' hEochaidh, 1977) Aside from population migration and stories traveling with the migrating people, phenomena involving fairy beings have been experienced in similar ways throughout ages on Irish and Romanian territories otherwise geographically isolated. Such experiences generated, and continue to generate, bodies of lore containing striking similarities woven within the uniqueness of each culture's folkloric patrimony. Most intriguing is the fact that such experiences keep occurring in modern times[40].

The parallelism between Irish and Romanian lore and traditions surrounding fairies can be summarized along the lines of a few marked differences, and many strong similarities.

Compared to the Irish counterparts, the Romanian fairies appear more prevalently connected to nature and natural phenomena, some taking form as nature-governing spirits. From among the zâne connected to the dead and those related to natural phenomena, some are acting as guardians for human communities (Pòcs, 2018). In Irish tradition, the aspect of fairies watching over a family takes on the expression of the ban sidhe announces the impending death of a family member.

Both Irish and Romanian fairy traditions mention the

crossover with the dead. The Rusalii, and their Queen Irodiada or Rosalia is celebrated on a holiday when the beloved departed ones are also celebrated and acknowledged with offerings. In Ireland human dead are sometimes encountered among the fairy, and An Dagda – god and king of fairies in Ireland – has also associations with the world of the dead.

The list of what zâne/iele and Na Daoine Maithe/ Aes Side have in common runs much longer, and includes: love of dance and music, party, food, and all pretty things; preference for euphemisms and titles; propitiation through offerings of dairy and bread, left by trees or places special to them; places or natural features that are known to be fairy abodes, and therefore out of bounds for humans. Also, both Irish and Romanian Fairy lore mention times and dates of heightened fairy activity which is felt in the human world, and therefore potentially dangerous.

Folklore in both cultures speak of fairies' interest in connecting with people they choose. Such people become gifted healers, musicians, poets, or good at divination and prophecy. Last but not least, zâne and Na Daoine Maithe both punish mercilessly and reward generously.

The abundance of common traits shall not misguide anyone into stating that Irish and Romanian fairies are the same beings; "Non idem est si duo dicunt idem."[41] It is not the purpose of this comparative study to whitewash fairies, nor sugarcoat their lore, infantilizing it to suit certain interests. Nor is the purpose of this book to level to the ground the differences between literary traditions in two distinct cultures and claim that fairies in Ireland and those in Romania are just the same. Just the opposite: similar experiences related to fairies as encountered in these two geographical areas, Ireland and Romania, invite pondering over the existence of other reasons accounting for such similarities. It invites pondering maybe to what degree fairy represent a phenomenon with more of a tangible reality to it than what modern society is willing to accept. Whether from

Ireland or Romania, alluring and scary, beautiful and eerie, magical, powerful, incomprehensible by human standards, neither entirely good nor entirely bad, they are fairies who elude logical thought. But this should not place their existence outside the realm of possibility.

Endnotes

40. Fairy encounters in modern times are mentioned in the Fairy Census compiled by Dr. Simon Young, recorded in the "Paranormal and Popular Culture" edited by Darryl Caterine and John W. Morehead, and "The Taming of the Fae: Literary and Folkloric Fairies in Modern Paganism" by Sabrina Magliocco, to name just a few.

41. Latin, "It is not the same [thing] even when people call [it] the same." The meaning in this case is that even when using the same list of descriptors, the discussion still addresses two different subjects. https://eudict.com

About the Author

Daniela Simina grew up in Romania, immersed in the rich local fairy lore. Since young, she apprenticed with her grandmother, a fairy seer and medicine woman. Walking into her grandmother's footsteps, Daniela became a medicine woman and fairy witch herself.

Daniela Simina is passionate about researching Irish and Romanian fairy folklore and traditions. She studied under the guidance of scholars and writers native to Irish culture, who are invested in preserving the historical and folkloric heritage. Daniela travels periodically to Ireland, to cultivate the connection with the Fair Folk in situ. In addition to writing, she teaches classes on energy healing and various esoteric subjects, including fairies.

From the Author

Thank you for purchasing "Where Fairies Meet". My sincere hope is that you found this book to be useful, and that you enjoyed it as much as I did while writing it. If you have a few moments, please feel free to add your review of the book to your favorite online site; I would be immensely grateful. Also, if you would like to connect with other books and events that I have coming in the near future, please visit my blog https://whispersinthetwilight.blogspot.com/ and website https://siminayoga.com for news on upcoming works, and recent blog posts.

Sincerely, Daniela Simina

References

Briggs, Katharine, "*A Dictionary of Fairies,*" 1976
Campbell, John Gregorson, *"Celtic Traditions,"*1900
Campbell, John Gregorson, *"The Gaelic Otherworld,"*1902
Caterine, Darryl, John W. Morehead *"The Paranormal and Popular Culture"*
Chelariu, Ana Radu, "The Most Prevalent Mythical Characters in Romanian Folklore", *Journal of Romanian Language, Issue 29/2021* retrieved at https://limbaromana.org/en/the-most-prevalent-feminine-mythical-characters-in-romanian-folklore/
Creangă, Ion, *"Harap Alb"*, 1877, published in the collection "Povesti," 2017
Daimler, Morgan "History and Meaning of the Word Fairy" https://lairbhan.blogspot.com/2020/08/history-and-meaning-of-word-fairy.html
Daimler, Morgan, *"Fairies. A Guide to the Celtic Fair Folk"*, 2017
Daimler, Morgan, *"Fairy Queens. Meeting the Queens of the Otherworld"*, 2019
Daimler, Morgan, *"A Modern Dictionary of Fairies"*, 2020
Daimler, Morgan, "The Witch, the Bean Feasa, and the Fairy Doctor in Irish Culture" *Air N-Aithesc*, vol. 1 issue 2, Aug. 2014
Detschew, Dimiter, *"Die Thrakischen Sprachreste"*, 1976
Dobrescu, Petre, "Legenda Babelor in Romania. Pietrele magice ale primaverii" 2020 https://www.libertatea.ro/stiri/legenda-babelor-in-romania-2161428
Dunn, Joseph, *"Táin Bó Cúalnge Translation"* release date August 7th, 2005
https://www.gutenberg.org/files/16464/16464-h/16464-h.htm
Eliade, Mircea *"Noaptea de Sânziene"*, 1955
Eliade, Mircea *"Occultism, Witchcraft, and Cultural Fashions: Essays in Comparative Religion"*, 1976

Eminescu, Mihai, *"Poems and Prose"*, 2017

Ghinoiu, Ion, *"Folk Almanac"*, 2005

Hele, Rodica *"Traditii si obiceiuri de Sânziene"*, 2020, https://www.academia.edu

Hele, Rodica *"Traditii si obiceiuri de Rusalii"*, 2019, https://www.academia.edu

Ispirescu, Petre, *"Romanian Folktales"*, 2016

Istrate, Ale "Mitologia Romaneasca vs Mitologia Greaca" www.academia.edu

Jones, Mary "Celtic Literature Collective" https://www.maryjones.us/ctexts/lebor5.html

Kligman, Gail *"Calus, Symbolic Transformation in Romanian Ritual"*, 1981

"Lebor Gabala Érenn, 65-95, https://www.maryjones.us/ctexts/leborgabala.html

Lenihan, Eddie, Carolyn Eve Green, *"Meeting the Other Crowd"*, 2003

Mawr, Elisabeth B., *"Roumanian Fairy Tales and Legends"*, 1861; reprinted Columbia

Press, 2021

Magliocco, Sabina, *"The Taming of the Fae: Literary and Folkloric Fairies in Modern Paganism"*, Magic and Witchery in the Modern West edited by Shai Feraro and Ethan Doyle White (Palgrave MacMillan, 2019)

Marshal, Ruth *"Clare Folk Tales"*, 2013, retrieved in electronic format at https://books.google.com

Mullarkey, Seamus, *"The Cats of Ireland: An Irish Gift for Cat Lovers, with Legends, Tales, and Trivia Galore"*, 2021

Muselea, O. Bârlea, *"Tipologia folclorului din raspunsurile la chestionarele lui B. P. Hasdeu"* 1970

O'Brien, Lore, *"Tales of the Old Ireland Retold"*, 2018

O'Brien, Lora, *"Fairy Faith In Ireland"*, 2021

O'Crualaoich, Gerald, The Book of the Cailleach", 2006

O'Curry, Eugen, translation *"The Faith of the Children of Tuireann"*

1863, retrieved at https://sejh.pagesperso-orange.fr/keltia/ version-en/tuireann-en.html)

O'hEochaidh, Sean, *"Fairy Legends from Donegal: Siscealta o Thir Chonaill,"*1977, retrieved at https://www.worldcat.org/ title/fairy-legends-from-donegal-siscealta-o-thir-chonaill/ oclc/610256485

Pócs, Éva *"Small Gods, Small Demons: Remnants of an Archaic Fairy Cult in Central and South-Eastern Europe"*, 2018

Pócs, Éva *"Fairies and Witches and the Bounday of South-Eastern and Central Europe"*, 1989

Rogers, Rosemary "Biddy Early: Witch or Healer" https:// www.irishamerica.com/2016/08/wild-irish-women-biddy-early-1798-1872-2/

Slavici, Ioan *"Stories"*, 2017

Spariosu, Mihai I and Dezsö Benedek, *"Ghosts, Vampires, and Werewolves. Eerie Tales from Transylvania"*, 1994

Stancescu, Dumitru, *"Basme Culese Din Gura Poporului"*, 1892

Stoica, Monica "Noaptea de Sânziene. Legende, Vraji si Traditii" https://www.mediafax.ro

Stokes, Whitley *"Cath Maige Tuiread"*, 1891 translation retrieved on https://celt.ucc.ie/published/T300011.html

Talos, Ion *"Petit Dictionaire de Mythologie Popular Roumaine"*, French translation by Anneliese and Claude Lecouteux, 2002.

Urechia, Nestor, *"Zânele din Valea Cerbului"*, 1904/1978

Vivod, Maria, *"The Fairy Seers of Eastern Serbia: Seeing Fairies-Speaking through Trance"*, 2018

Wilde, Lady, *"Irish Cures, Mystic Charms & Superstitions, 1826-1896"*, reprinted 1991

Williams, Noel, *"The Semantics of the Word Fairy: Making Meaning Out of Thin Air"*, 1991

Young, Simon, Ceri Houlbrook *"Magical Folk: Fairies 500 AD to Present"*, 2018

"Muma Pdurii si Alte Spirite in Folclorul Românesc", 2020 http://mythologica.ro/muma-padurii-si-alte-spirite-in-folclorul-romanesc/

Irish Imbas, "The True Story about the Fianna", https://irishimbasbooks.com

MOON
BOOKS

PAGANISM & SHAMANISM

What is Paganism? A religion, a spirituality, an alternative belief system, nature worship? You can find support for all these definitions (and many more) in dictionaries, encyclopaedias, and text books of religion, but subscribe to any one and the truth will evade you. Above all Paganism is a creative pursuit, an encounter with reality, an exploration of meaning and an expression of the soul. Druids, Heathens, Wiccans and others, all contribute their insights and literary riches to the Pagan tradition. Moon Books invites you to begin or to deepen your own encounter, right here, right now.

If you have enjoyed this book, why not tell other readers by posting a review on your preferred book site.

Recent bestsellers from Moon Books are:

Journey to the Dark Goddess
How to Return to Your Soul
Jane Meredith
Discover the powerful secrets of the Dark Goddess and
transform your depression, grief and pain into healing
and integration.
Paperback: 978-1-84694-677-6 ebook: 978-1-78099-223-5

Shamanic Reiki
Expanded Ways of Working with Universal Life Force Energy
Llyn Roberts, Robert Levy
Shamanism and Reiki are each powerful ways of healing; together,
their power multiplies. *Shamanic Reiki* introduces techniques to
help healers and Reiki practitioners tap ancient healing wisdom.
Paperback: 978-1-84694-037-8 ebook: 978-1-84694-650-9

Pagan Portals – The Awen Alone
Walking the Path of the Solitary Druid
Joanna van der Hoeven
An introductory guide for the solitary Druid, *The Awen Alone* will
accompany you as you explore, and seek out your own place
within the natural world.
Paperback: 978-1-78279-547-6 ebook: 978-1-78279-546-9

A Kitchen Witch's World of Magical Herbs & Plants
Rachel Patterson
A journey into the magical world of herbs and plants, filled with
magical uses, folklore, history and practical magic. By popular
writer, blogger and kitchen witch, Tansy Firedragon.
Paperback: 978-1-78279-621-3 ebook: 978-1-78279-620-6

Medicine for the Soul
The Complete Book of Shamanic Healing
Ross Heaven
All you will ever need to know about shamanic healing and how to
become your own shaman...
Paperback: 978-1-78099-419-2 ebook: 978-1-78099-420-8

Shaman Pathways – The Druid Shaman
Exploring the Celtic Otherworld
Danu Forest
A practical guide to Celtic shamanism with exercises and
techniques as well as traditional lore for exploring the Celtic
Otherworld.
Paperback: 978-1-78099-615-8 ebook: 978-1-78099-616-5

Traditional Witchcraft for the Woods and Forests
A Witch's Guide to the Woodland with Guided Meditations and
Pathworking
Mélusine Draco
A Witch's guide to walking alone in the woods, with guided
meditations and pathworking.
Paperback: 978-1-84694-803-9 ebook: 978-1-84694-804-6

Readers of ebooks can buy or view any of these bestsellers by
clicking on the live link in the title. Most titles are published in
paperback and as an ebook. Paperbacks are available in traditional
bookshops. Both print and ebook formats are available online.

Find more titles and sign up to our readers' newsletter at
http://www.johnhuntpublishing.com/paganism
Follow us on Facebook at https://www.facebook.com/MoonBooks
and Twitter at https://twitter.com/MoonBooksJHP